PRAISE
FOR FOLLOW THE DRAGONS

"Kyle has gone through hell and kept going. Surviving an abusive childhood, he turned to drugs and then to crime. Defying odds, he pulled himself out of the dungeon and became a success. But the happy ever after never followed. His success brought only more hollowness and despair. So he threw away the good life and headed west in a converted cargo van in search of real happiness. The adventures that followed are wildly inspirational and uplifting. His transformation was as improbable as it was extraordinary and I found myself cheering for him every step of the way."

—DEAN KARNAZES, ultramarathoner, one of *TIME Magazine's* 100 Most Influential People in the World and nationally best selling author of *Ultramarathon Man*

"*Follow the Dragons* is honest, gritty and real. It's Kyle's story of mental, emotional and physical endurance. His courage to authentically share the trials and tribulations on his path is inspiration to us all to run through life challenges and face our own demons."

—KATIE SPOTZ, youngest person to row solo across the Atlantic and author of *Just Keep Rowing*

"A harrowing and gripping adventure. Kyle's dramatic story shows what's possible when someone is able to confront, and overcome, their past to achieve the impossible. A must read!"

—MARSHALL ULRICH, bestselling author of *Running on Empty*

"Kyle delivers a riveting tale of personal adventure and struggle. His honest and open-hearted assessment of his own character flaws made me cheer, hoping with every page turn that he would find his way to the mountaintop. *Follow the Dragons* is a book that will keep you reading late into the night."

—CHARLIE ENGLE, ultrarunner and author of *Running Man*

FOLLOW THE DRAGONS
DISCOVERING THE LOVE OF
ULTRA RUNNING AND MYSELF

KYLE V. ROBINSON

Town-B Press

Copyright 2018 © Kyle V. Robinson
All rights reserved.

Published in the United States by Town-B Press
Town-B Press and the Mountain Footprint design are trademarks of Town-B Press, LLC

This book or any portion thereof may not be reproduced or used in any manner whatsoever without the express written permission of the publisher except for the use of brief quotations in a book review

ISBN 978-1-7327703-0-0
eISBN 978-1-7327703-1-7

Follow the Dragons: Discovering the Love of Ultrarunning and Myself / by Kyle V. Robinson

PRINTED IN THE UNITED STATES OF AMERICA

Cover design by Andy Bridge
Interior design by Phillip Gessert

10 9 8 7 6 5 4 3 2 1
FIRST EDITION

AUTHOR'S NOTE

Writing this book I relied on journals, photographs, texts, emails, and my own recollection. I have changed locations and the names of individuals, modified identities and details when necessary to preserve anonymity. The dialogue in the book was created from my memory that evokes the feeling and meaning of what was said at the time. Everything written in the book is as accurate as possible and based on the truth as I experienced it. The views expressed are my opinions.

TO KATE AND KIRK

CONTENTS

PREFACE — xi

CHAPTER 1
FATHERS: MOTHER DOESN'T ALWAYS KNOW BEST — 1

CHAPTER 2
THE VAN: HOME IS WHERE I PARK IT — 17

CHAPTER 3
THE MEETING: TWO'S COMPANY, THREE'S A CROWD — 31

CHAPTER 4
HIGH SCHOOL: DRUGS, FIGHTING, AND LAWYERING — 47

CHAPTER 5
WASHINGTON STATE: WHEN YOU CAN'T BEAT 'EM, JOIN 'EM — 65

CHAPTER 6
COLLEGE: NEW FRIENDS, SAME OLD STORY — 85

CHAPTER 7
LAKE TAHOE: NOTHING IS AS IT SEEMS — 101

CHAPTER 8
SAN FRANCISCO TO LAW SCHOOL: WHEREVER I GO, THERE I AM — 121

CHAPTER 9
MOAB: I THINK WE'RE ALONE NOW — 135

CHAPTER 10
NYC: I GET BY WITH A LITTLE HELP FROM MY FRIENDS — 153

CHAPTER 11
EUGENE: FAMILY MAN 171

CHAPTER 12
GOING ULTRA: FORWARD GROWTH 183

CHAPTER 13
GOODBYE: I THINK I'M ALONE NOW 197

CONCLUSION 209

ACKNOWLEDGEMENTS 211

PREFACE

It was early September, the sun would soon be going down, and I was almost ten thousand feet above sea level on a single track trail near South Lake Tahoe running as fast as my legs would carry me. With every stride, my breath became increasingly labored. Glancing down through the tall pine trees as I climbed higher and higher above an empty ski resort parking lot, I could see the eastern shore of Lake Tahoe glistening in the sun and the casinos and hotels in the basin of Stateline, Nevada. I wasn't dressed properly for the weather that was coming, wearing only my blue running shirt and black running shorts. Although it was close to seventy degrees at the moment, I knew the temperature could quickly drop to below freezing once the sun faded behind the mountains. I hadn't thought I'd be out on the mountain this long, but there I was, still going, because Tim was lost, and somehow it had become my responsibility to find him.

Mile four turned into mile five, which turned into mile six, and so on, as I ascended the hill. The farther I ran, the more frustrated I became. *How could he get lost? The course is well marked, and it's still daylight. Where the fuck are you, Tim?*

A few hours earlier, we had received word from Adam, who was tracking Tim, along with every other runner participating in the ultra-marathon race, that Tim was off course. Way off course. All the runners were equipped with a spot tracker, which they kept attached to their running packs at all times so that Adam at race headquarters could track them via satellite. If runners were in trouble, they were able to call for help with the spot tracker by pressing a distress signal button. That, in turn, would let race HQ know, and hopefully, someone would be able to locate and rescue them.

"The spot tracker has Tim, bib number forty-seven, off course. He's pressed the emergency distress button three times to signal for help," Adam had said, his voice echoing through the radio.

I could hear his distress, and I imagined his thumb turning white from all the blood rushing out of it as he pressed down hard on the two-way radio button to communicate with Robin, a volunteer coordinator, on the other end.

Robin, Debbie, and I were standing next to each other outside a canopy tent at an aid station, where the runners could refuel and get some rest, on the eastern side of Lake Tahoe. "*What?*" she said, her voice tinged with concern. "What do you mean?" Runners were only supposed to signal for help in a dire emergency. If the emergency button was pressed, we had to consider it a life-and-death situation.

"We have a runner who is off course, lost, and needs help. His last check-in was at the ski resort aid station a few hours ago," Adam said again, this time more urgently.

Debbie, the race director, turned to me, put her hand on my shoulder, and said, "We have a serious problem."

"Right. We need to go get him," I responded without hesitation.

Robin agreed.

Apparently, Tim had gotten to the aid station after cutoff—the point at which the aid station closes and runners aren't permitted to continue their race. Not only that, but Tim also seemed a bit out of it and delirious when he arrived. Hearing this, Debbie, was furious that the aid station captain not only let Tim leave in the state he was in, but also permitted him to go on after the cutoff time. Aid station captains were supposed to inform race HQ of any runner who arrived past the cutoff time, and HQ would help make the decision of whether to let the runner continue or inform them that their race was over. But Race HQ hadn't been told and Tim, after resting for a bit at the aid station, had left without telling a soul.

We also learned that Tim had gone off the trail in the dark the previous night and made a few wrong turns, which is not uncommon when racing an ultra-marathon. A race this long may take several days to finish, and runners need to be able to navigate in complete darkness at times and might even need to take sleeping breaks.

The good news, though was that Tim was less than eight miles from another aid station. According to his spot tracker, he kept turning around and heading in the opposite direction every few miles, indicating he didn't have any idea where he was or where he was going. Because of his frequent turnarounds, we were concerned that he might not be lucid and wondered if he was properly fueled or just simply lost.

We had no way to communicate with him—we could only see where he was and where he was going. We had no information about his food or water supply or if he had proper clothing with him. Both Robin and I knew Tim—he was an experienced long-distance ultra-runner, running distances well over 26.2 miles (the marathon distance) on a regular basis—and this fact eased some of our concerns.

We immediately contacted the El Dorado County sheriff's office and informed them of the situation to see if they could help us with the search-and-rescue mission. However, things weren't dire enough just yet from their point of view. Technically, he wasn't missing and there were no reports of him being in serious danger.

Once we realized the local authorities were going to be of minimal help, we took matters into our own hands. We were going to rescue Tim as soon as possible.

As much as I actually wanted to save Tim, I also wanted the challenge and the distraction. Being an experienced trail runner myself, it made sense for me to go after him. In fact, I had run along the exact trails Tim was now lost on not even a week earlier, when we were marking out the race route. When I told Robin and Debbie I was going after him, they agreed right away and handed me a two-way radio so I could stay in contact with them and Adam. I jumped into my van and took off on Route 50 towards Tim's last location, barreling down the road. I only had a few hours of daylight left. I hoped I could run up the trail, find Tim, and bring him back safely and be a hero.

The aid station I was at was about a forty-five-minute drive from the ski resort aid station, where Tim had last checked in. When I arrived there, it had been closed for hours, and was completely abandoned aside from a dozen trash bags, folded-up tables, and the head medic, Larry, who had already been informed about what we knew of Tim's condition. He'd been expecting me.

Larry was a heavyset guy who always wore his red medic shirt with the white cross on the front and back. He loved being a medic and was always concerned about every runner, but in this particular case, I could see the anxiety written all over him: sweat beads stood out on his forehead, his voice was unusually serious, and he was working hard to maintain a calm and collected demeanor. Seeing me, he opened the trunk of his brown Subaru station wagon and asked if I needed anything. In the cargo space, there were, among other things, a bottle of water and a granola bar. I grabbed them both and stuffed them into my pocket. We agreed that Larry would wait for Tim and me there unless he heard otherwise.

Time was of the essence; I had to find Tim before nightfall. The lower the sun sank into the horizon, the higher the chance was that he would have to spend the night in the woods, potentially putting his health in danger. Nodding goodbye to Larry, I raced up the hill, the two-way radio in my left hand and the bottle of water in my right. My adrenaline was already pumping.

I stayed in constant contact with Adam over the radio as we tried to pinpoint Tim's exact coordinates. Unfortunately, he was moving farther and farther away from the ski resort parking lot, where I'd started. My hope of finding him within the first thirty minutes quickly faded. I cruised up the mountain following the trail I had previously marked. Ski lifts towered above me, tall pine trees stood to my left and right, and dry, light-brown dirt crunched under my feet.

Before I knew it, I had covered over seven miles. Considering that Tim already had over seventy miles on his legs from this race, he was moving surprisingly quickly. According to Adam on the other end of the radio, I wasn't gaining much on him, and I was growing frustrated.

Finally, in the distance, I saw a few people on the trail. *Maybe it's Tim*, I thought hopefully. There wouldn't be many hikers this deep into the trail this late in the day; perhaps someone else had found him and was helping him.

Once I got closer though, I saw that this was not the case. Instead, they were just a couple in their early forties.

"Have either of you seen a runner with trekking poles and a small backpack who looked lost?" I inquired, trying to catch my breath.

"Nope. We haven't seen anyone in quite some time," the woman responded.

I relayed this information back to race HQ, and it was not received well. *Where the hell are you, Tim?*

I briefly explained the situation to them, and the hikers were kind enough to offer me more water. I hadn't anticipated being out there this long, and I had already consumed the granola bar and most of the water I had brought with me. Thanking them, I continued on, running farther up into the mountains and screaming Tim's name as loudly as I could.

Tim was tall and lanky. In his real life on the coast of Oregon, he was a high school counselor. I'd gotten to know him and his wife, Pam, on a previous adventure in Washington State. He was an accomplished ultra-runner in his own right and wasn't a stranger to the trails or to this race. Tim's experience was comforting, but it was also concerning, because he normally wouldn't have put himself in such a dire situation. He knew better.

As time passed and I went farther up the trail, I was starting to get concerned for myself. I lacked proper clothes and supplies, and as I ran deeper into the mountains, the two-way radio became increasingly spotty. The dense pine trees now blanketed the landscape, and all I could hear was my breath, my feet pounding along the trail, and coyotes howling in the distance. I was more than ten miles into my search—way beyond my and HQ's expectations. The sun was getting low, and so were my chances of finding Tim. At some point, I would eventually have to decide whether to turn back or keep going.

The course was well marked with reflective neon-orange and neon-pink ribbons on clothespins to help runners find their way even in the dark. When the sun went down, the runners could still see a sea of reflective ribbons on trees, rocks, and bushes with their headlamps. To runners on an ultra-marathon course, these ribbons—which we call "dragons"—are their entire life. Without them, they really might die. I knew the course was well marked, particularly in this area, because I was the one who had helped mark it. All Tim had to do was follow the dragons on the trail. It was so easy. So why couldn't he do it?

As I flew along the trail, I considered the irony of the fact that I was the one on this rescue mission. It's not that I wasn't capable of running and finding Tim in the middle of nowhere. No, what was ironic was that I had never been able to follow the course markings in my own life—the life I was still trying to escape. All I'd had to do in life was follow the dragons that were so prominently displayed. But I hadn't. Instead, I so often chased after the wrong ones or missed them completely. For years, I had assumed I was going in the right direction, but I was wrong. I thought that if Tim had known this about me, he might have wished it were someone else chasing after him. Even though I knew exactly where I was going on the trail, I felt more lost than I ever had in my life, and now, someone else's life was in my hands.

My thoughts were interrupted by Adam's static-laced voice over the radio: "Kyle, if you don't see Tim in the next mile or so, just head back."

I stopped running for a moment and looked up at the empty trail, feeling somewhat defeated. I pressed the radio button to reply, "I'm not coming back without Tim."

I pushed forward without knowing the outcome, as I always do.

CHAPTER 1
FATHERS
MOTHER DOESN'T ALWAYS KNOW BEST

In 1983, I was four years old and lived on the left side of a lime-green duplex in Kent, Ohio. Ronald Reagan was president, Michael Jackson was the biggest star in the world, and break dancing was all the rage. Well, at least it was in my neighborhood. I often saw kids walking around with ripped-up pieces of cardboard boxes they had taken from the dumpster at the end of our street so they could bust a move wherever they were. I wasn't quite old enough to break-dance, but I was able to watch in awe and appreciate the amateur dancers from my front-row seat on my red-and-blue Big Wheel bike.

Late one weekend afternoon in early October, I was playing with my favorite stuffed animal, Wicket from *Star Wars: Return of the Jedi*, in my room upstairs. I unexpectedly heard the doorbell and the sound of Mom opening the front door. A man's deep voice greeted her. *This is new*, I thought. It wasn't every day that someone showed up at our door. Curious, I raced downstairs to investigate.

When I arrived at the bottom of the stairs and didn't see anyone, I expanded my investigation. I turned the corner to head toward the dining room and on into the kitchen. As I entered the dining room, I froze in my tracks, my heart pounding. Standing before me was a towering figure. This giant stood well over six feet tall and was much larger than an average man. He sported a thick brown beard and a pair of bifocal glasses. My eyes traveled farther down to see he wore a green T-shirt and a beat-up brown Carhartt jacket. In his left hand was a clear plastic bag containing a carton of chocolate marshmallow ice cream. His right hand was tucked into his jacket pocket.

Mom was in the kitchen, and my brother and sister were still playing upstairs. Alone with this giant stranger, I greeted him as any kid would greet such a large, intimidating man—with a punch in the leg. I giggled, but for only a moment. The next thing I knew, a clenched fist the size of a softball flew out of this man's pocket and toward my stomach. It was like getting struck by a Mack truck going over seventy miles per hour. I keeled over in pain and gasped for breath, begging my lungs to start working again. Tears ran down my cheeks like a waterfall. I couldn't scream because I still couldn't breathe. It didn't matter anyway; nobody was coming to help me because nobody knew what had happened. I grabbed the corner of the daisy-patterned tablecloth that was on the dining room table, which looked more like a curtain, and used it as a tissue.

This huge man looked down at me and did not apologize. He didn't try to comfort me. He just stood there, watching me. He probably thought I'd gotten what I deserved for punching him in the leg for no reason. Afterward, I started to think that maybe I *did* deserve getting punched in the stomach.

I was only four years old, and this was my first meeting with my stepfather, Ben, or as I later referred to him, "Triple B": Big Bad Ben. This first meeting was pretty indicative of how our relationship would go.

Our green duplex was on Silver Meadows Boulevard. Years later, I'd learn that our street also bore the local nickname "Silver Ghettos Boulevard." It wasn't exactly the nicest area. I didn't know any better as a kid, and it didn't matter if we lived in the ghetto or Beverly Hills. Back then, that duplex was all Mom could afford. My uncle owned the home, so I'm sure she was getting a good deal.

By the time Triple B came along, it was me; my sister, Kate, who was a year and a half younger than me; my brother, Kirk, who was two years older than me; and my twenty-nine-year-old mother. My mom had been divorced for less than a year, and she was desperately seeking a father for her three kids. Our biological father was completely out of the picture, and my mom didn't want him *in* the picture. She didn't think he was a good father and said she never felt loved by him. But of all the men Mom could have met at the local community center singles' night mixer, she probably couldn't have picked a worse candidate to bring home than Triple B.

Like most kids, I was always looking for ways to have fun. I wanted to interact with everyone, to make them laugh and smile. I was curious. My life goal at that point was to be happy. And I couldn't understand why people were any other way. Until, that is, Triple B appeared in my life like a guest unwanted by everyone except Mom. It seemed to me that Triple B wasn't a happy person. In fact, I think he was the most miserable person I've ever met. He didn't laugh and didn't joke, unless it was the occasional off-color joke, and he just complained about life and how everything and everyone was the worst. Traffic was his mortal enemy, every driver was out to ruin his day, and nobody could drive worth a lick, except him. He'd pull up to a light, trying to turn left, and announce that "every goddamn person and their mother" was out on the road that day, ruining his drive.

In hopes of lightening his mood and seeing a smile through his scruffy beard, I would often make jokes. "Why did the skeleton go to the movies alone?" I asked one day from the backseat of our early-eighties brown Chevy station wagon. "Because no-*body* would go with him," I said, providing the punch line to my own joke and cracking myself up in the process.

Triple B just glared at me in the rearview mirror through those dense bifocals of his with a look that said, "Stop talking. You're an idiot." To him, everyone was terrible and an idiot. He was the only one justified in having an opinion.

A few months after Triple B came into our lives, early one morning, Mom woke us kids up and instructed us to put on our church clothes, even though we wouldn't be attending Mass. Mine consisted of worn blue corduroy pants and a yellow polo shirt. We then piled into the station wagon and headed to the local courthouse so Mom could marry Triple B. Even though she was a devout Catholic and never missed a Sunday service, they weren't getting married in a church. I assume they didn't want to go through the trouble and expense of a real church wedding because it was the second bite at the apple trying to be husband and wife for both of them. My mother's first marriage had been annulled by the Church—giving her the freedom to marry again. Only us kids attended the ceremony, and we sat on wooden pews in the gallery. Too young to understand what was going on, I joked with my brother about the silly man with a mustache wearing a black dress who was presiding over the ceremony. I quick-

ly quieted down though when Mom glared at me, telling me to be good with only her eyes.

In addition to Mom's three kids, Triple B had two children of his own from his previous marriage: a six-year-old boy and a nine-year-old girl. They were going to live with us. Creating this sudden large family forced Triple B and Mom to make some decisions in order to support us. They determined that the best course of action was for Triple B, whose education had stopped when he dropped out of college early, to enlist in the navy. He became a machinist's mate and worked on the water pumps aboard ships. Being in the navy was not just a job; it was an adventure. At least, that was their slogan at the time. I didn't think the adventure applied to the servicemen's families, and I definitely didn't know that "adventure" really meant "nightmare."

Being a military family meant we had to move every four years. Our first stop on this navy "adventure" was Philadelphia. Philadelphia in the mid-eighties wasn't exactly the safest place. At least, it didn't seem that way to me. We lived in navy enlisted housing on base, which were basically run-down condominiums. The homes were just row upon row of the same connected units, all painted the same bland light yellow. There was nothing special about them. Walls as thin as paper separated us from our neighbors, and I could repeat everything they discussed at their dinner table each night word for word. In turn, I'm sure the neighbors could hear the constant screaming and yelling on our side, especially when Triple B got home. I could easily smell the cigarette smoke or the aroma of meatloaf through the vents from four or five units down.

We also didn't do anything to make our home any better than it was, and no one could ever have mistaken Mom and Triple B for clean freaks. With seven people in the house, there was an endless amount of dirty dishes piled up in the sink, and it was always the kids' responsibility to clean them. I wouldn't be surprised to learn that Triple B actually had a phobia of warm water and dish soap, because he never once washed a dirty plate in over twenty-five years. However, he did seem to be an expert on how the dishes, pots, and pans should look when we were done washing them. I know this because he would inspect them, and if they were not up to his standards—and they rarely were—he would be furious, and we'd feel his anger in the form of a physical or verbal assault.

Because the kids were in charge of the dishes, it stood to reason that we would be expected to clean the rest of the house as well. Every child had assignments that rotated on a weekly basis. For example, my brother might be on dishes, my sister on dusting and vacuuming, and I would be on TC & F (table, counters, and floors). Because children were left in charge of cleaning, the drains were often clogged with week-old pasta, the refrigerator smelled, and tables were covered in dust more often than not. It wasn't rat infested or a total disaster area; it was just always cleaned half-assed.

What was a disaster though were the Philadelphia public schools. Due to all the horror stories I heard, I was under the assumption that if I even stepped into one, it would be the end of me. Think of all those heartwarming movies where the school's a wreck before the lead character comes in and cleans it up, straightens all the kids out, and kicks out the riffraff. Those were the public schools in Philadelphia at the time. Graffiti covered the lockers, kids had to walk through a metal detector every day to get in, fights broke out on a regular basis, and kids cruised down the hallways on dirt bikes. Okay, maybe not dirt bikes, but I know that image isn't too far off.

Fortunately, I was able to dodge that bullet by attending a Catholic school called Holy Spirit. Mom insisted on it, in fact. Triple B wasn't crazy about paying for private school, but he wasn't crazy about anything. They were only able to afford it because they got a break on the tuition since Triple B and my mom were sending so many kids there, and because of their meager income.

To help out with the finances, Mom, who lacked a college education as well, took odd jobs depending on where we lived. She was a librarian in one place and a school lunch monitor in another. Mom would eventually earn her degree while I was still an adolescent and become a histologist. She was the person who identified cell types and placed microorganisms on slides for doctors to examine.

Mom loved being a mother. She loved her children to death and would have done anything for them. Unfortunately, that love was also the reason Triple B was in our lives; she felt it was essential that my siblings and I had a father. In her spare time, she would bake, sew, and make quilts. She made quilts for all the kids' beds before they were ten. She made me feel like I was the best, and she loved all her kids that way. She even went so far as to make a shirt for me with "Kyle the Best" ironed on it. I was the only one who had such a shirt, which made me feel special. I wore that shirt constantly, and I believed I truly was the best kid ever born because of her.

I loved going to school because I loved being anywhere Triple B wasn't. I'd get up early in the morning, put on my uniform—black pants, a maroon sweater, and black shoes—head downstairs, and pour myself a bowl of Life cereal or whatever had been on sale that week at the grocery store. Then I'd head to the bus stop with my siblings. We all took the bus to and from school each day because by the time we left, Mom would already be at work, and of course there was no way Triple B would ever give us a ride.

Besides, even if it had been possible for them to take us to school, they wouldn't have. It was the kind of thing that didn't even occur to them: they got themselves to work, and we got ourselves to school. They didn't do it to teach us responsibility, it was just something they didn't care about.

Once at school, I would sing my heart out in choir and play four-square at recess. If I arrived early enough, I would go to the Mass they held in the rectory next to the school. Scattered throughout the pews would be a few older women and a nun or two. When I was a kid, I wanted to be a priest when I grew up, so part of me thought I needed to be at Mass all the time. However, thoughts of joining the priesthood quickly subsided once I hit puberty and found out just what celibacy meant.

Every winter, the school choir would travel to the local mall and perform a concert of Christmas carols. We all wore Santa Claus hats and belted out "Silent Night" to the crowds trying to get their last-minute shopping done as Sister Collette, my third-grade teacher, did her best impression of a conductor. Sister Collette was a stereotypical nun: a short, older lady who always wore the full Roman Catholic habit.

Outside of home, it seemed like I had a "normal" childhood. I played soccer and baseball, and I was even the pitcher on my T-ball team—now, that is an accomplishment! I loved being with my friends and playing sports. Mom came to every single one of my games and cheered me on, screaming, "Knock the cover off the ball!" Triple B never once attended any of my games.

At home, I lived in perpetual fear of upsetting Triple B. It was like constantly walking on eggshells. At dinner, if we put our elbows on the table while we were eating, he would stab us in the arm with his fork. Then there was the stick that Triple B nicknamed "Big Red." Big Red was a piece of smooth wood about eighteen inches long and one and a half inches thick. At some point in its past, it had been spray-painted red. There was the outline of a dozen or so clothespins on the stick because it had been used as a background for one of our school projects, for which we needed to spray-paint clothespins for some reason. The stick was always conspicuously displayed so all the children knew where it was. If we upset Triple B in any way, which didn't take much, the stick would come out.

One time, when I was eight years old, I was watching TV with my brother and sister after dinner. I was tired and accidentally fell asleep on the chair with my head on the armrest. I was drooling a bit, and the drool got on the chair. I was rudely awoken by Triple B grabbing my shirt and ripping me off the chair. I looked up and saw him snarling in rage, yelling, "You're a fuckup! How many times have I told you not to do that?"

He threw me around like a rag doll until he felt certain that I was far enough away from the chair. I ended up being tossed against the wall in the hallway, under a framed picture of a lighthouse. "Don't fucking move," he told me.

I was shaking with fear and knew where this was heading. He came back with Big Red, and I started screaming for Mom to help me. She in turn was already yelling at him, begging him to stop. But nobody could stop him in that house. We all wished we could. That night, I went to bed with sores and bruises all over my legs from a few stick lashings. Still, the fear of being hit by Triple B was worse than the actual beating.

Seeing the children she loved so much in pain hurt Mom dearly—I know this. She would witness our beatings with terror and tears in her eyes. She had asked him to stop, to no avail. But what more could she do? She didn't want another failed marriage on her hands. She rationalized that it wasn't that bad, that Triple B would change, or that things would get better. Plus, she thought that having a father figure in the house was necessary for raising a family, that having a physically and emotionally abusive father was better than having no father at all. All Mom wanted was a father for her children; instead, she got a miserable monster who just wanted to be by himself or around other like-minded miserable people.

Unfortunately, Triple B's anger and rage didn't stop with us kids, and he and my mom fought a lot. Neither of them knew how to be in a relationship; they just thought they had to be. One time, on our way home from a trip to the store, Mom and Triple B were screaming and yelling at each other in the car. I couldn't stop crying because I wanted everyone to just be together and be happy. Triple B was threatening divorce, and as much as I was afraid of him, I didn't want him to hurt my mom's feelings.

As we arrived home and got out of the station wagon, Mom took my hand. I was in tears and asked her if everything was going to be okay. Triple B got out of the driver's-side door, still screaming at Mom. She asked him to tell me, a frightened, crying eight-year-old boy, that everything was going to be okay. He refused. He just walked into the house and told us to fuck off.

After that, I never looked forward to seeing him—ever. I prayed that he would just change, go away, or die. Every time he came home, I was afraid. All of us kids would hide in our rooms when Triple B got home and simply wait for Mom to call us to dinner.

From the start, Mom tried to force a relationship between us kids and Triple B. She made us call him "Dad" and referred to him as our father, which only made me not want to call him either of those things. Plus, I already had a dad, albeit maybe not a great one. But I knew my biological father existed, would see him once or twice a year, and got cards from him on Christmas and my birthday.

I got the feeling that Triple B didn't care whether or not I called him "Dad"—he certainly never asked me to. He never did any of the standard fatherly things: he never took me to sports games, never played catch with me, never talked to me about girls, never taught me how to shave, never asked me how I was doing, never hugged me, never apologized to me for anything. There was no bonding of any kind. He called me names a lot—"loser" was his favorite. Our relationship was characterized by fear. I was afraid of him, and to him, I was just an annoyance. We had no connection.

Years later, as an adult, back in Ohio one afternoon, I was in the car with Triple B while he was running an errand, and we ended up taking a back road. As we drove down the twisting narrow road, we came upon a red covered bridge that had clearly been built in the late nineteenth century. As we passed it, Triple B pointed it out. "I proposed to my first wife on that bridge," he said.

"Oh yeah?" I responded, not knowing where this was going.

"It collapsed the next day," he continued. "I should have known from that that my marriage was going to fall apart."

That's odd, because when you walked into my house when I was only four, my whole life collapsed, too, I thought to myself.

This was the gist of most of his stories: he was always the victim of shitty situations. He told these stories to excuse his unacceptable behavior.

It took me a long time to realize that not all men were like Triple B. Throughout my adolescence, I was somewhat afraid of every man I met, because I assumed they were all miserable people, too. It was like an epiphany when I discovered that half the world wasn't full of Triple Bs. At first, I was confused and shocked, unable to digest this new information. My entire world was turned upside down, and it changed my way of thinking. *Maybe I don't have to live in fear for the rest of my life. Maybe I can choose to be happy.* Whatever I was going to be, I wanted to be the opposite of Triple B, and I was willing to do whatever it took to become that.

Right before we moved away from Philadelphia when I was around nine years old, my grandmother died in a car accident in Ohio. In many ways, her death broke my mother. They had been very close, and Mom was never the same again. I was heartbroken, too. My grandmother was someone I always felt safe with, enjoyed being around, and knew loved me. I had no idea what she thought about Triple B but would surmise she knew my mom could have done better. I know she wouldn't have been pleased with the way he treated us or my mom.

After Grandma's death, Triple B never once comforted me or even asked how I was coping. I don't remember him comforting Mom, either. Mom fell apart at the funeral and actually fainted. Triple B just watched the whole thing from the back of the funeral parlor, not talking to anyone.

When we moved to Newport, Rhode Island, right after Philadelphia, in 1989, there wasn't any navy housing available, so we were forced to rent a furnished home until space opened up on base. We moved into a place that was less than a mile from the ocean, but it was also run-down, and I had to share a bed with my brother. By this time Triple B's kids had moved back with their mother.

In Newport, Triple B's beatings became more frequent, and he increasingly turned his abuse toward Mom as well. He'd scream and yell at her as if she were a child.

Mom made dinner for the family every night, and she was a decent cook. One summer evening, when I came in from playing outside, I smelled the Italian sausage frying in the cast-iron skillet and the garlic bread baking in the oven, and I knew in an instant that we were having spaghetti for dinner—one of my favorites. The only problem was that Triple B wanted something different that evening. He wasn't in the mood for spaghetti, and he let Mom know about it. He had been blaming her for his weight gain lately, and he thought that the spaghetti in particular was contributing to the extra pounds he'd been putting on. Of course, he also refused to eat anything healthier.

As my mom dished out the sausage onto Triple B's plate, he swatted the spoon away with his hand and sent the sauce-covered meatball flying across the kitchen. He stood up, towering over my mom, and she backed up toward the open doorway that led to the basement stairs in fear. Spaghetti sauce dripped onto the floor from the spoon she still held.

"You want me to eat this shit and get fat?" he screamed in her face, almost shoving her down the stairs.

In tears, Mom grasped the side of the doorway with her free hand as all us kids looked on from the dinner table without a word. We were terrified. Suddenly, Triple B backed off, sat back down, and started eating as if nothing had happened. I was crying inside.

I never actually witnessed him slap or punch my mom, but that doesn't mean that it didn't happen. But I did witness the emotional abuse—there's no question about that.

I now wonder why my mom didn't think she deserved better. Why didn't she think her kids deserved better? I guess it was hard for her to realize that because she was holding out hope that he would change or that things would get better—but they didn't. Shouldn't there be a point where enough is enough? It's easy to look at others' decisions and second-guess. It's harder to be in the moment and still hope. Instead of leaving, my mother started pretending and rationalizing.

To deal with all the pain and uncertainty I felt at home, I needed an outlet beyond just sports. I started to interact with other families, searching for the happiness I wasn't finding in my own home. I was constantly over at our neighbors' houses, looking to hang out, even if they didn't have kids. I simply wanted to be around happy people.

Mom brought Triple B into our lives with the best of intentions, but the situation got away from her at some point. She showed me and my siblings love on a daily basis; she just wasn't equipped to deal with whatever Triple B was.

I assume Triple B didn't know any better about how to raise a child. He didn't know how to be a father or how to love a kid. He was the way he was because of how he was raised: by an abusive father who disciplined with corporal punishment. I guess history really does repeat itself, and as is so often the case, abuse has a way of trickling down from generation to generation.

Still, I couldn't help but wonder what it would be like to have a real father. Mom always told me that my biological father was terrible because he wasn't around. I, in turn, always thought that not being around was much better than the emotional and physical abuse I received from Triple B.

Despite all of Triple B's shortcomings, there were a few silver linings to having him in our lives. He exposed me to camping. He didn't teach me how to start a fire or pitch a tent, but he took us to campsites on occasion. He was slightly involved in the Cub Scouts with me, but only because Mom made him. Living on the naval base, I was able to see all kinds of battleships. We would often travel around the country to visit old Civil War battle sites and see interesting historical places like Williamsburg, Virginia, or Gettysburg, Pennsylvania. Triple B would never explain why these sites were interesting or important—it was more for his curiosity—but at least I got to see them. Finally, an unintended consequence of Triple B's abuse was that it brought me closer to my brother and sister; being treated like crap by Triple B was something we all had in common.

After fours year in Philadelphia and four years in Newport, Triple B retired from the navy, and we moved to

Cuyahoga Falls, Ohio, which is about forty-five minutes south of Cleveland. I was in the seventh grade at the time. The good news was that we were finally done moving around. The bad news was that I was getting old enough to really rebel and act out.

As I got older, the physical abuse became less frequent, but the mind-twisting, all-out emotional abuse hurt more than I could have ever imagined, and it was more than I could handle. Being raised on daily doses of fear and abuse for eight years would have dangerous consequences now that I was coming of age.

CHAPTER 2

THE VAN
HOME IS WHERE I PARK IT

"Are you really going to buy this?" Brad asked. A tall, handsome, sensible fellow with thick brown hair, he was seriously questioning my admittedly rather wacky, and seemingly impulsive, decision.

I'd known Brad since seventh grade, and he was one of my oldest friends. We were standing in the parking lot of a car dealership, staring at a silver 2012 Ford Transit Connect cargo van shimmering in the hot July sun in 2016. After a few minutes, I simply replied, "Yes."

I had committed to being in the Cascade Range in Washington State—almost 2,500 miles away from my current home in Cleveland—in less than two weeks. At that time, this van would essentially be my new home.

I had done my research on the van. And by "research," I mean I looked at a lot of Ford Transits for sale online and had test-driven two others. Businesses used these vans for everything from electrical work to delivering flowers. The cargo space was six feet long, four feet wide, and a little over four feet high. It's perfect for hauling small loads or, as I was going to do, building a bed in the back and living in it.

There is an entire community of people who live in vans, and doing so is especially popular in the western

United States and Australia. Living in a van allows people to explore the world in a way that doesn't cost an arm and a leg and gives them a sense of freedom. I was craving both. Plus, why camp when I could literally just sleep wherever I parked? If I got tired, I could just crawl in the back and go to bed. It seemed simple.

I needed to get out of Ohio and get out quickly. Otherwise, I knew I'd be stuck in the ordinary, "successful" life I had created for myself there. And I couldn't live with myself if I did that. I thought this trip would fix everything that was wrong with my life. *It's now or never, Kyle,* I told myself. *If you don't get this van, your life will be the same as everyone else's. Who cares if you're going to be thirty-eight years old and living in a van?* Admittedly, I cared, but I also knew it was society's norms telling me it wasn't the right thing to do. I was going to do it anyway. I bought the van.

To be fair, I felt uneasy when I signed for the van. My heart was beating rapidly, and I felt pain twist the pit of my stomach. *Don't sign,* a voice in the back of my head warned. I almost got up and left the dealership at one point. *This isn't a smart decision. You're trading in a fully paid-off car. You don't need this van. Your life is going well, Kyle. This doesn't make any sense.*

But there was also a part of me that was scared of what would happen if I didn't buy the van. *You can't live the life you've been living. This version of success is not fulfilling. It's not you. There is still more out there in the world that you need to explore. You have this opportunity. Take it!*

By all accounts, I was a success. Even after stumbling early in life, somehow I had managed to become a licensed attorney and run a thriving business. However, despite all I had accomplished, I still wasn't fulfilled. I still thirsted for more. I didn't feel like a success, and I definitely didn't feel like I was being true to myself or doing everything I was capable of. I wanted to be happy, and my career wasn't making me happy. I thought this van adventure was the solution to my unhappiness.

Plus, I wasn't completely running away from my life. I was able to travel because the company I had created was entirely online, giving me the freedom to still make money without being chained to a desk. Some professionals must take courses in order to maintain their licenses or professional credentials, and I provided those certification courses through a website. All I needed was an occasional Internet connection and access to a phone.

Also, call it lucky or unlucky, but I didn't have a significant other, a child, or even a pet to spend my time with. It was just me. Most of my friends in the area had real jobs or families. Not many had a lot of time to spend with a bachelor, nor did they want to, for that matter. If my friends did want to hang out, the only thing they wanted to do was drink. And by "drink," I mean get really drunk.

I spent my Sunday mornings and afternoons drinking at either the Winking Lizard Tavern—a converted Elks lodge—or Merry Arts Pub and Grille, where all the townies could be found. The bars would be packed with sports fans getting drunk, screaming at the TV, and watching their favorite team—usually the Cleveland Browns—lose.

On one such day though, I needed a change. I grabbed a round of tall Budweisers from the sticky bar and brought them back to the table. "Here ya go," I said, setting the bottles down in the center of the table. "I'm leaving after this round. I don't want to sit here all day and get wasted."

"Why? Don't be a loser. You have nothing better to do," said short, chubby, and bald Chris as he gulped his beer and slammed the bottle back down on the table.

Yeah, my friends were the kind of people who called their friend a loser. I had long since gotten used to hearing the insult.

I didn't want to get in an argument, but at that moment, I felt like anything would be better than sitting in that smelly bar with them all day, getting blackout drunk and munching on free popcorn. I couldn't explain to them that I knew this wasn't what I wanted out of life; they wouldn't have understood, nor would they have been willing to understand. I didn't feel like the drinking or the drinking-related camaraderie added any value to my life. Plus, I felt like shit the next morning, and I didn't like who I was when I got really drunk with them. I'd say or do things that I would regret in the morning—things I definitely wouldn't have done sober. I hated it and I hated myself for doing it.

My usual Sunday-morning drinking comrades were Chris and Tommy. Tommy was a heavyset fellow who was always in the mood for a joke, though he didn't give me as much shit as Chris. If I ever tried to engage them in a conversation about life or about becoming a better person, I would get shot down for "being weird." They just wanted to talk about getting laid, making money, and making fun of other people. When we went out, the main point wasn't to watch the game; it was to get drunk. I went along because I "didn't have anything better to do," which was just bullshit, I told myself. I used it as an excuse to avoid doing the work to become who I was truly meant to be. I was afraid of who that was and what that would look like—what if it wasn't all it was supposed to be?

This particular Sunday was different. After I set down the beers, I looked around at all the people in the bar drinking and staring at the TV and thought to myself, *This isn't living*, I stood up and told Chris and Tommy I was going to the restroom. I didn't want to explain to them I was actually leaving. I didn't want to hear it from them and I knew they really didn't care, as long as I bought my round of drinks. I left the bar with thoughts of buying the van dancing in my head.

I knew there were people out there doing more with their lives, doing the things I wanted to be doing. I saw these people on Instagram running trails, climbing mountains, or just constantly traveling. I understood that social media was no basis for evaluating my life and that it was something of an illusion. Still, it made me realize that there was an entire world to explore and that I wasn't taking advantage of it. And what was I doing instead? Drinking at the bar or lying on my couch watching *Game of Thrones* or reruns of *Law and Order*, and knowing that there was much more to life than what I was experiencing. I would tell myself, *You're wasting your life. There has to be more to it than my couch, TV, and boozing with friends.* But was I actually going to do something about it?

Even though I was lucky enough to have the opportunity to just go on an adventure, it still took me some time to actually give myself permission to do so. When a door is open, it can be surprisingly hard to walk through it, especially when what's waiting on the other side is unknown. The doubts crept in: *You're thirty-eight; this isn't what thirty-eight-year-olds do. You should be buying a house and starting a family. You still have to pay rent; you can't just leave and pay rent on a place you're not living in. You won't be able to focus on your job as much. You might not have Internet access everywhere you go. You don't even know where you're going. This is not a sound decision. How are you going to meet a girl when you're not settled down? This trip is something you need to plan for a long time. What will people think?*

I grew up hearing these voices, the ones that constantly said, *You're not good enough. You're not one of the lucky ones. You can't do that. That's not possible. Get a good job, get married, buy a house, have kids, and that's life.* I didn't listen—I rarely did. That was how I had usually lived my entire life: I would hear the doubts and either pay no attention to them or let them fuel me to do the impossible, just to prove I could.

Even after I bought the van, I still didn't have a solid plan; going out west was as far as I had gotten. I didn't know how long I would be gone. I knew I would eventually have to come back to Ohio, because I had an apartment there with my belongings in it. Though, to be fair, all I really had of value was my TV and bed, two of the things I was trying to get away from.

When I thought about the trip and what would make me happy, I always came back to my love of trail running and ultra-marathons. An ultra-marathon is any race whose distance is longer than 26.2 miles. Some common ultra-marathon distances are 50 kilometers (31.1 miles), 100 kilometers (62.2 miles), 100 miles, and even 200 miles. Because these types of races don't bring big crowds or money, it's more of a community of runners helping each other out than a competitive environment. Ultra-marathons can take place on any surface—road, trail, or track—though trail running was my preferred way to go. I think, subconsciously, part of the attraction was that everyone who ran ultras, including myself, was looking to run as far away from their problems as possible and ultra-marathons gave us this opportunity.

What could be a better way to explore nature and find my tribe than spending some time around ultra-marathon races? Being out on the trails filled my heart with peace and excitement. Plus, all the best trail races are out west, and they're always looking for volunteers to work aid stations, handing out food and water; organize parking; check runners in; mark the course; and so on. Volunteering at races would give me a destination, something to do, and a way to meet people who were in the same community. My decision was made: I would volunteer at an ultra-marathon race out west and meet my peeps.

As I searched for volunteer opportunities with ultras, I came across a race in the Cascade Range in Washington State, specifically in the Gifford Pinchot National Forest. This wasn't a typical ultra-marathon; this race took place near the iconic Mount Saint Helens. The race started at Mount Saint Helens in the Cascades and finished in Randle, Washington, traversing the mountains.

It wasn't a stage race, either. Stage races are divided into several parts, or legs, and may have more than one participant on a team doing a leg. They often take place over the course of several days or even weeks, with rest days built in for the participants. This race, on the other hand, was a solitary nonstop run. All runners got when they finished was a belt buckle and the satisfaction of completion. There was no prize money or fanfare. That was part of the appeal.

The race in the Cascades was looking for volunteers to help mark the course and help out with the race. Races that take place over long distances, especially on trails, need to be well marked beforehand so runners don't get lost. The marking is done by "fast packing"—circumnavigating the entire route with a backpack as fast as possible to place flags, markers, dragons, stakes, and signs to direct the runners along the course. Course marking was an ideal option for me because I would get to see the entire course and the surrounding landscape and also get some exercise. It seemed like exactly the kind of adventure I was looking for.

I emailed the race director, Debbie, and she put me in touch with other volunteers, Paul and Robin. I offered to help out at the race and told them I'd meet them in Washington in late July or early August. They quickly emailed me back and accepted my offer to come mark the course. They informed me they would already be course-marking by the time I arrived in Washington and I should plan to meet them on the mountain. We would rendezvous at Elk Pass, a trailhead near Mount Saint Helens, about forty-five minutes outside of Randle.

I bought the van shortly after I emailed Paul and Robin and two weeks before I left to meet up with them. Before I left, though, I needed to convert the van so that I would be able to sleep in it whenever I wanted. This process can prove to be both crazy and expensive. People often turn these vans into literal homes, with running water, ovens, microwaves, and toilets, and they spend tens of thousands of dollars doing this conversion. I would have loved to do that—though without spending the money—but I had less than two weeks. Also, I wasn't exactly sure what I wanted, other than a bed. I told myself that once I got out west, I would figure out what I really wanted in the van and build accordingly. I knew I wouldn't need a sink with running water, as I had a few gallon jugs. I didn't need a toilet, as I had a pee cup, and to take care of other business, I'd just stop somewhere or hold it. I had no need for an oven or microwave—I had food that didn't need to be cooked, and I could always stop somewhere along the way. All I really needed was a bed, a book, my journal, my phone, and my computer.

I found plans for an easy bed conversion online and decided to just go with that. I went to my local Home Depot and bought a bunch of wood and supplies. I feel it is important to note that I do not have one handy bone in my entire body. The good thing is that I can follow directions well, so I hoped these two facets of my personality would balance out.

In the end, the bed I built was nothing spectacular, but it worked. It was basically a wooden box frame that was a little over six feet long and two feet wide. It was about a foot and a half off the floor so I could store supplies underneath it. I also had the foresight to build an extender on the bed in the event I would need more sleeping space for a guest. That wooden bed was where I would be sleeping for the next five months.

The final step in the van-conversion process was to shade or black out the windows. Although the windows were already factory tinted, prying eyes could still see into the van if they really wanted, and I needed more privacy if I was going to make this my home. I bought a roll of reflective insulation and cut it up to fit the shape of each of my windows. Then I spray-painted the reflective pieces black, so when they were against the window, it would look like a very dark tint job and no one could see inside. I also purchased a retractable curtain rod, placed it on the ceiling right behind the front seats, and hung an old set of blue curtains to block the view from the front of the van. With that, my van conversion was complete.

I did, however, still lack in one area: supplies—mainly camping gear. After a few weeks out west, I did finally figure out what was necessary and eventually made a trip to REI, but before that, my initial stock included: a Walmart tent borrowed from my brother, a goose-patterned 1960s sleeping bag, a two-gallon cooler, a Walmart butane camping stove, an assortment of camping dishes, a battery-powered fan, two duffel bags of clothes, and my running gear. I also had five pairs of shoes—two pairs of road-running shoes, trail shoes, casual shoes, and walking shoes—and a Styrofoam cooler. I would quickly regret not bringing my thermal jacket. Because it was summer when I left Cleveland, I didn't realize how cold it could get in the mountains in the Pacific Northwest.

In late July, 2016, I packed up, fueled up, and took off, heading west in my van. Driving cross-country from Ohio to Washington alone was a nightmare. According to Google Maps, it was a trip of 2,425 miles, taking thirty-five hours. With sleep, it took me almost two full days. The directions took me through the northern parts of the United States via Interstate 90. I was alone, and I wished I had someone to talk to during those hours and hours of driving along the not-so-scenic highway.

Early in my journey, I drove past Chicago and saw the city's skyline with the formerly named Sears Tower in the distance. I thought of all the suits going to their nine-to-five jobs and smirked. It wasn't until I hit Wisconsin that I began thinking, *What the hell are you doing, Kyle?* I tried not to dwell on that thought though and just kept pushing forward. I had a goal: to make it out west to meet Robin and Paul.

Around two in the morning, I pulled into a rest stop to get some shut-eye in the van for the first time. As I looked out through the mosquito-covered windshield, I could see the moon and a few stars scattered through the clear night sky above. It was a warm night—close to eighty degrees—and the rest stop was surprisingly packed with weary travelers. I searched the lot for a good spot, as I didn't want to park right under a lamppost or too close to the busy building. I quickly learned that the prime sleeping spots are at the very end of a rest area exit. I was lucky enough to grab one of those coveted spots when I saw a green jeep pulling out. After parking, I grabbed my Dopp kit and went to the bathroom to brush my teeth.

Brushing my teeth in a rest stop as the guy to the left of me was taking a leak was an odd experience, as was having strangers coming and leaving as I was going through my nightly routine.

That night, I met a guy in his early twenties with long black hair and a poor excuse for a mustache towing a cartful of kittens. He was in the bathroom cleaning out one of the cat's cages.

"Where ya heading?" he asked me.

I looked up, took the toothbrush out of my mouth, and said, "Washington State. You?"

"I'm from Wisconsin, and I gotta get these cats to my girlfriend in San Diego. You'd be surprised how much they shit on the drive." This was exactly what I wanted to hear as I was brushing my teeth. He continued, clearly wanting to have a conversation at two in the morning in a rest-stop bathroom. "Washington State, huh? That's a hell of a drive," he said, hoping I'd say something in return.

I just nodded and started to pack up my things. "Good luck," I said, leaving the bathroom. As I headed toward my van for the night, I thought again, *What the hell am I doing?*

I had a tough time trying to sleep that first night, thanks to the noise from the tractor-trailers. Their engines ran all night, even when stopped, and I could hear the drivers entering and exiting the rest stops.

As I put in more windshield time, I saw North Dakota: its wheat fields, cattle ranches, and strip malls. In Montana, the sky seemed to go on forever, as did the state itself. I saw a few miles of Idaho, and then, finally, I was in Washington.

I was getting close to my destination, but there was a slight hiccup: I hadn't heard from the race volunteer coordinators in a few days, even after repeated attempts to contact them. I wasn't alarmed, because I knew there wasn't any cell reception on the mountain, but I wasn't sure where exactly to meet them. They were moving all over the mountain, and although we had agreed to meet at Elk Pass, there was also a possibility that they either hadn't arrived yet or that they had arrived and had already left.

As I got closer to Randle, lush evergreens covered the landscape on either side of the two-lane highway. The shops, strip malls, and gas stations gave way to trees, mountains, cabins, and wildlife. As the environment around me turned greener and greener, the signal on my cell phone got weaker and weaker.

I drove through the city of Packwood, which is east of Randle, and stopped at a gas station to fill up and get some beer, so as to not show up empty-handed. As I left the gas station and headed on toward Randle, suddenly, the RV in front of me slammed on its brakes. I came within inches of hitting the bikes attached to its rear bumper. I looked ahead and quickly saw the reason for the abrupt stop. A majestic dark-brown elk was crossing the road without a care in the world.

You're not in Ohio anymore, Kyle.

I finally entered Randle and passed the church on my right. That's where the race was going to finish and where our headquarters were.

Randle was a small town, consisting of three restaurants, a handful of churches, a grocery store, the junior high school, the high school, a public library, and a campground. Luckily, I had cell reception, so I entered the coordinates for Elk Pass that Paul had given me and headed up 131 for our rendezvous.

Although Elk Pass was only about twenty-five miles from Randle, it took over forty-five minutes to drive there. At 6,700 feet above sea level, the road started to get sketchy. There were several potholes and washouts. The van was not made for this type of driving, and I started to wish I'd purchased a vehicle that was higher off the ground and had all-wheel-drive capability. Eventually, I lost cell reception.

As the road finally crested, I saw a brown sign on the right with yellow letters that read, "Elk Pass." I pulled into the trailhead parking and spotted a red Silverado 1500 extended-cab truck with stickers all over the back that indicated different ultra-races. I knew I was in the right spot and a sense of relief washed over me—I had arrived.

Nobody was with the truck, so I knew they were still out course-marking. I was exhausted and I decided to take a nap while I waited for Paul and Robin to return. I snuggled up with my sleeping bag and tried to get some shuteye.

CHAPTER 3
THE MEETING
TWO'S COMPANY, THREE'S A CROWD

A few hours after midnight, I woke to the sound of a dog barking and a truck door slamming. I looked out the window of my van to see a light mist of rain falling. Through the raindrops, I could see a lanky fellow with a thin brown beard, who looked to be in his late thirties, fumbling around in the back of the Chevy truck. He wore a trucker hat backward with a headlamp strapped to his noggin. *This must be Paul.*

As I got out of the van to greet him, his dog, which looked like some sort of black-and-white husky/Labrador mix, started barking even louder. Evading his dog, I reached out and shook Paul's hand.

"Shut up, Gus! Sit! He's harmless," Paul said, gripping my hand firmly. "So you're Kyle? Thanks for meeting us. How long have you been waiting?"

"A few hours, but I needed the sleep, so it worked out," I replied, trying to escape Paul's grasp.

"Want some food or beer?" He nonchalantly took the bottle cap off his IPA with a Bic lighter.

"No thanks."

"Robin should be along soon. I'm actually surprised I beat her here." He sounded more impressed with himself than surprised.

Paul had just gotten done marking seventeen miles of the course. To kill time as we waited, he pulled out a map of the Gifford Pinchot National Forest and laid it across the hood of his truck. He pointed out our current location and explained our plans for the course-marking process, tracing trails and roads with a highlighter so I could follow along, and he detailed how many miles we would be doing each day, how long it was going to take, and where we would be sleeping each night.

As Paul talked, he polished off a first and then a second IPA. The whole time, he kept looking in the direction Robin was supposed to be coming from. She was marking fifteen miles of trails and should have been back by now.

Finally, out of the blue, Paul shouted, "*Marco!*" Again, "*Marco!*" He waited a solid minute and then yelled a third time, "*Marco!*"

In response, we heard a faint, "Polo!" It was Robin.

In the distance, I saw a light floating in the darkness. Finally, I saw the body attached to the headlamp come into full view. "You must be Kyle," she said as she put out her hand to shake mine.

I took it and nodded. I wasn't really interested in conversation; I was so out of it from my drive and the time change that I just wanted to go back to bed.

Robin was short, thin, and outfitted in rain-running gear, but I couldn't make out much of her other features due to the darkness around us and her headlamp shining in my eyes. She sat down and proceeded to drink a beer, eat, and throw pieces of her sandwich towards Gus to keep him at bay. I later learned Robin is highly allergic to dogs and was always doing her best to keep her distance from them.

Before I crashed on my makeshift bed, they let me know that the next day's plans were not set in stone, which was good, because I had to get up early and go back into town to access the Internet for work.

I would soon learn that the people involved in volunteering for ultras out west were a group of ultra-runners who lived in the woods in their cars or tents during the race. They would spend weeks, sometimes even months, setting up for a race. They were a tribe, and their way of life was sometimes affectionately known as living the "dirtbag life."

I knew that going into town every day would not be realistic—at least, not if I was going to be a useful volunteer. Plus, it wasn't feasible, as some days we would be over three hours away from civilization and cell reception. We had over a hundred miles of remote trails to mark, and we needed to get it done soon. They didn't have time for a city slicker like me to be going into town every day to check his email and make phone calls. So now that I was out here, I needed to arrange for someone else to answer customer inquiries when I wasn't around.

With that thought, I went to bed. Paul slept in his truck, I in my van, and Robin in her car.

I woke well before the others the next morning at around five forty-five. It was cold, the sky was gray, and the clouds hung low, hovering just above the trees. I raced down 131 toward Randle through the potholes and washouts. Finally, I pulled into the parking lot of Mt. Adams Cafe at the bottom of the hill and turned on my hotspot Internet device; I was in business. I called a friend who had previously agreed to cover for me and gave her a brief crash course on what she needed to do for my work. It wasn't complicated. Once I had reliable

Internet access in a day or two, I would again be able to take care of any issues or questions customers had. This was something I definitely should have taken care of before my adventure. Luckily, I got it covered just in time.

When I returned to the site, Paul and Robin had just gotten up; I was relieved that I hadn't held them up. Paul was sitting in a green camping chair, sipping coffee, and Robin was standing at the back of the Chevy with the tailgate down. A Jetboil was lit in front of her, and she was waiting for it to heat water for her coffee. It seemed like nobody was in a hurry to get the day started. Stuffed under her trucker hat, Robin had short blond hair. He skin was tan from being outdoors so much. She had a tattoo of a sitting Buddha on her right forearm and an outline of a mountain range on the back of her left calf. She had hazel eyes and the whitest teeth when she smiled.

"You get done what you needed to get done?" she asked me.

"Yep, I'm ready to course-mark," I replied happily.

"Want some coffee?"

"Nope, I grabbed some while I was in town."

At that, Robin began explaining the day's plan. It was evident that she knew exactly what she was doing, and that we were just along for the ride. In turn, Robin and Paul could tell right away I had never done anything like this and that I was new to the dirtbag mountain life. Fortunately, they were patient and willing to show me the ropes. I was eager to learn.

"We need to pack our bags for the day first," Robin said. "Do you have a pack?"

I went over to my van and pulled out a small backpack that was big enough for a book and a computer. "Will this work?"

Robin started laughing. "No. I think we have an extra one you can borrow, though." She handed me a big gray backpack that was over five times the size of the one I had pulled out.

She put fifteen wooden stakes into my pack, which we would later pound into the ground with a hammer. "When packing, stakes go in first—unless you're a vegetarian, that is." She laughed at her own joke.

"Next are the signs," Robin continued. These were reflective signs with arrows on them, which we would staple to the stakes to point runners in the right direction whenever it was necessary, like when there was a fork in the road or if it was unclear which trail to take. I added twenty of these reflective signs to my pack.

"Now put the dragons in on top."

At this point, the dragons were on a rope called a "pom-pom." The pom-poms would go around our bodies like a sash or hula skirt so we could easily attach the dragons to the course. We carried five pom-poms each: four in our pack and one around our body. There were probably 150 dragons on each pom-pom. In the near future, I would become very familiar with dragons, as I would be making hundreds of them.

"Finally, you need enough food and water for the trail," Robin said as she continued to pack the bag. We made peanut butter and jelly, and cheese and honey sandwiches and packed several candy bars, along with water. Lots of water—two to three liters per person. When it was all said and done, my pack weighed close to forty pounds.

With our bags packed, the next item on our agenda was figuring out the logistics of course-marking: shuttling our cars around and deciding what needed to be marked, who was going to mark what, who was going to end up where, how we were going to get back, and where we were going to park the three vehicles.

Evidently, before I showed up, there had been another volunteer who lived nearby, but he'd left because Paul and Robin were fighting too much about logistics. I didn't feel like I had the option to just leave because I was so far from home and had invested a lot of money and energy in this adventure. Anyhow, I didn't really have anywhere else to go. Also, after my childhood, being around people who were constantly fighting was something I was used to.

I told them that if I ever got in the way, they could have Debbie fire me. Robin responded that she would never fire a volunteer. Apparently, I took that as a challenge.

First, we shuttled Robin's car out to where we were all going to meet and dropped it off. Then, we piled in Paul's truck and drove to a trailhead about twenty miles away to drop Robin off so she could start marking and head to the rendezvous point where her car was parked. Paul, Gus, and I then drove in the opposite direction towards the Lewis River campground where we were going to start. We'd leave Paul's truck there and pick it up later. All this was so all three of us would end up at the same place when we were done marking.

Once Paul and I reached the Lewis River, we strapped on our packs and set off to mark. It was slow going at first because I had no idea what I was doing. Paul had to tell me where to clip the dragons on the trees and where to staple a sign or hammer in a stake. I watched him in his orange-and-blue-striped tank top place a dragon seemingly at random or take one of mine down, trying to understand the method.

Making things more difficult was the fact that we were traversing the course backward. That is, we were marking in the opposite direction from the way the runners would be going. Therefore, every time we put up an arrow, we had to turn around and be sure it was facing the right direction. I was surprised at how many times we had to adjust the arrows.

Paul described himself as a mountain-biking bum and found odd jobs when he could. Robin worked as an online marketer and was able to work remotely giving her the freedom to volunteer at races. Paul told me how he had met Robin a few years back when he was out on one of his adventures. Paul was cool, funny, and easygoing, the kind of guy who was nice to everyone unless someone crossed him—and even after that, he might still give them the benefit of the doubt.

As we were heading up the trail, without my asking or any context, Paul told me that Robin was his wife. This statement seemed strange, because they slept in separate cars, didn't wear wedding rings, had different last names, showed no affection toward each other, and fought a lot. I didn't think much of it at the time, but I realized that he wanted me to have that information for a reason. I also learned Robin had a son from a previous relationship who lived with his father.

We saw very few people on the trail and even got lost a few times. After the first time, I realized that this was the norm; getting lost was just part of course-marking. Luckily, we were equipped with a high-powered GPS with the trail marked on it, so we could navigate our way back. Of course, that was only if the GPS was accurate and fully charged. Sometimes, it was neither.

Whenever we did run into other people on the trails, we had to explain ourselves and what we were doing for several reasons: 1) as a couple of guys running or walking down the trail with a bunch of neon ribbons wrapped around our bodies and large packs strapped to our backs, we definitely looked odd; 2) we needed to let people know that the markers were for an actual purpose so they wouldn't take them down; 3) we had to let people know we weren't crazy or stoned; 4) people were just curious; and 5) some of these people hadn't seen another human on the trail for quite some time, and it was simply nice to talk to them and learn why they were also out there and where they were from.

I was surprised by how many people would want to sabotage someone's race by taking down the course markings we were putting up. It was mostly people who thought we were denigrating the serenity of the forest or teenagers pulling a prank. I wasn't really surprised by the latter group though, because I probably would have done the same thing when I was a teenager if I had seen the markings. Of course, it would have been a better prank if they turned the arrow signs to point in another direction and then placed the dragons going in that direction instead, leading runners down a different path, as opposed to just taking the markings down. That would really have gotten a lot of runners lost. Truly, these kids were prank amateurs.

I spent the next few sunny days marking with Paul, and then at night, we met Robin back at camp. We were all friends having a good time. Whoever returned to the campsite first had to make dinner and have it ready for the others when they arrived. It made the whole process into a challenge, a race, and a goal to shoot for. No matter when we arrived though, seeing the cars at the end of the day gave us an amazing feeling.

My first few outings marking the course with Paul were quite the experience. I saw snow-capped Mount Adams and the blown-off summit of Mount Saint Helens. The trails were a lot narrower and very technical with an abundance of roots, rocks and other obstacles, making them much more dangerous than the ones I was used to in Ohio, and the elevation was like nothing like I had experienced before. There were times when I looked down into the valley hundreds of yards below and the only thing that prevented me from going over the edge was my own balance.

Not only did I get to see great landscapes and amazing scenery, but we also met a few interesting people. On our second day of marking, Paul and I entered a clearing and saw a white late-sixties VW bus with the paint chipping off the side. As we walked over to investigate, we found a man in his mid-forties with thinning black hair and a clean shave standing in front of a deer hide about the size of a bedsheet stretched between the trees.

Paul took the lead. "Hey! Whatcha doing?"

"Oh, man! Hey, guys, welcome! My name's Dan." Dan appeared to be very excited to see us. "I'm getting this hide ready. I'll be wearing it for the ceremony."

"What ceremony?" Paul asked.

Dan pointed up the hill in the direction opposite to where we'd come from, where there was no path. "Vision quest. Up there. We built a sweat lodge. I'll be leading the quest. That's what this hide is for."

At the time, out in the woods, this seemed like a reasonable explanation. Now, not so much. Still, Dan seemed like the happiest guy in the world as he prepared his deer hide.

The next day, as night was approaching, I was waiting for Paul to meet me back at the truck when a green Ford Ranger pickup pulled up beside me. Inside was a couple in their early thirties, and they were ready to party.

A young woman with a black ponytail and a white, midriff-baring tank top exited the truck and asked me if I had a pump she could borrow to inflate their air mattress. They would be camping there for the night. I grabbed our pump from the truck and handed it to her.

"What's your name?" she asked.

"Kyle. You?"

"I'm Tetris Superstar. Nice to meet you," she replied, and did some kind of odd curtsy. "We have some mushrooms. Would you like some?"

I laughed and declined her offer. That was the thing about being out in the middle of nowhere: anyone could be whoever they wanted to be, and nobody questioned it.

Later that evening, we went by Tetris Superstar's camp, and we could hear the music blaring from a distance. There were a few more cars at their site now, and they had set up a disco light, which was illuminating the forest canopy, spinning and changing colors. It looked amazing. I suppose Tetris and her beau were on their own kind of vision quest. I should have told them to meet up with Dan.

After several days course-marking, we needed to go back into town to get supplies and prepare to meet up with Debbie and some other volunteers who'd be helping mark the rest of the course. The mere mention of going back into town was music to my ears; I would be able to check in on work and clean myself up a bit. I hadn't showered in almost a week, and I knew it was even longer for Robin and Paul. I couldn't remember the last time I had gone that long without a shower, but I didn't really mind because we were all in the same boat. We decided to stay at a local campground in Randle—Cascade Peaks—so we could shower, have a fire and a few beers, and wait for the others to meet us the next day.

The plan was for me to go into town earlier alone so I could reserve the campsite and pick up some packages that had been sent to race HQ. While I was in town, Robin and Paul finished marking a section of the route.

In town, I secured the campsite, picked up the packages for Debbie, took care of my business, and took a shower. Robin and Paul completed course-marking early enough to join me for a late lunch.

I met them at our favorite spot, Mt. Adams Cafe. I arrived first, and then Paul joined me. He slid into the booth across from me, facing the cafe's entrance. Paul had changed into a red-and-black flannel shirt with gray stripes throughout. He wore flannel often. We both had our laptops out and were enjoying a cold IPA while we waited for Robin.

When she finally arrived and walked up to our booth, she paused for a moment, as if she were waiting for me to move over so she could sit beside me. I didn't move. After what Paul had told me on the trail about their marriage—or, more accurately, after what he didn't tell me about it—I knew he was sensitive about Robin. I didn't want to give him the impression I was interested in her, at least not blatantly. I was trying to play it cool but felt he suspected something was afoot.

Instead, Robin plopped down next to Paul, facing me. I closed my laptop to give her my full attention. She had cleaned herself up a bit since I saw her last. I'd never seen her with makeup on before—in fact, this was the first time I had seen her not covered in dirt on the mountain. She wore her usual trucker hat but, this time, her short, blond hair wasn't tucked up, it fell an inch or two past her ears. I could see her hazel eyes clearly, and I noticed a hint of freckles on her face.

In that moment, I felt happy and content as we ate lunch and talked about the past few days on the trails and what was coming up. This was exactly what I had come out here for: to spend time on the trails and meet new friends.

Paul spent most of the meal hunched over his laptop watching mountain biking videos on YouTube and laughing to himself while Robin and I talked. This was the first time we had been indoors together, sitting at a table, and actually relaxing. The smell of trees and musty tents had been replaced with burgers, coffee, and beer. I still felt like a newcomer and my insecurities started getting the better of me. Maybe they felt I wasn't really an outdoor trail runner. I was trying to let them know that I was part of their tribe too. I didn't want to be exposed for the fraud I feared I was.

This feeling was only amplified by the fact that they were both sitting across from me like I was at a job interview being evaluated and judged. They weren't treating me badly, but I so desperately wanted to prove to myself and to them that I belonged. So, when the bill came, I grabbed it and paid for the whole thing. It seemed like the least I could do. After all, they had been feeding me over the past few days and teaching me about course-marking, camping, and surviving outdoors.

But when I made that gesture, which I had intended to be one of camaraderie, Robin looked over at me with her stunning hazel eyes and smiled. It was much more than just a regular smile, though—it was "the look," and I knew it. I'd seen "the look" a few times before from other girls.

I was momentarily taken aback. *Is she interested in me?* I wondered. Aloud, I simply said, "What?"

"Nothing. It's just nice of you to buy us lunch. It's really cool," she replied. "Isn't that right, Paul?"

"Yeah," he said under his breath, still staring at his computer. I sensed that Paul knew something strange was going on between us and that he wasn't happy about it. I also suspected he'd experienced this with Robin before and knew the signs.

It was late afternoon by then, so we left the cafe to head to the campground, have a few beers, and relax. More volunteers would be showing up the next day, and we would get access to the shed at the church where we would have our race headquarters. We needed to be ready for the next stage of preparation.

The campsite was basically an open field where we could park our vehicles, set up a tent, and have a fire. However, none of us needed to set up tents because we were all sleeping in our vehicles. We set up a few camp chairs, and I retrieved firewood from the campground store. We started a fire, and the three of us began drinking.

Eventually, Paul retired to his truck. He had a cot set up in the cab. He turned his radio to a classic rock station, which I think was meant to drown out our talking; left the back of the cab open; and went to bed.

Then it was just Robin and me hanging out by the fire. We drank even more and started talking about serious things, like our lives and careers, money, and what we wanted out of life. She didn't mention her relationship status with Paul and I didn't ask. Paul was far enough away—the vehicles were parked about twenty-five feet from the fire—that he couldn't possibly hear what we were saying, especially with his radio on. We eventually ran out of wood, so we decided to find more and started tearing down small trees nearby, laughing and getting closer as we worked together.

Once we sat back down and had the fire going again, Robin leaned over toward me. I could see the reflection of the fire flickering in her eyes. She put her hand on my leg and said, "I'm really attracted to you." Although I'd heard her the first time, I made her repeat it because I liked hearing those words. "I'm really attracted to you," she said again.

I felt the same way, but I didn't say anything. I just leaned over from my cheap blue polyester camping chair and kissed her. We continued kissing for a long time. The fire went out again, but things were just heating up between us.

I stood up, took her hand, and led her over to the side of my van. I suppose this was also a way to get farther from Paul, as Robin's car was parked next to his, and my van was parked on the other side of hers, but I didn't consciously think about that at the time.

Robin leaned back on the van, and I pressed my body against hers. The smell of our fading campfire was now faint in the air. We weren't being that loud, and the only thing I could hear was our occasional bumping into the side of the van as we kissed each other in the darkness. If anyone had been looking our way, they would have clearly seen two figures in the moonlight really enjoying each other's company.

"Would you like to get in the van?" I finally asked.

"Yes," was her simple reply.

I took her hand once again and led her toward the back of my van. The doors were already open, so we crawled inside, and I closed them behind us. The smell of the musty goose-patterned sleeping bag, which was spread out on the wooden platform, immediately replaced that of the campfire. I briefly considered pulling up the extension I had built to make the bed bigger but quickly abandoned the idea once inside.

Afterward, as we were getting ready for round two, we heard a loud banging on the outside of the van. I turned my head to look out the back window. I hadn't put up the privacy shades because I didn't have time and didn't think of it. As a result, I could now see a shirtless, skinny, pale Paul standing in the moonlight, banging on the van, and yelling, "Robin! *What the fuck?!*" It was probably my closing the van doors that had tipped him off. I have to give him credit, though; at least he didn't try to open the door. He patiently waited for us to get out.

Oh shit, I thought. Robin and I were half dressed, and I wasn't in the mood for a fight. Robin didn't say anything; she was busy looking for her shirt, which was buried somewhere in the sleeping bag. It took us some time to gather ourselves and get the rest of our clothes on. Then I opened the back of the van, and Robin and I hopped out.

Paul was incensed. He didn't look at me, though, he just yelled at Robin. "What the fuck?! What the fuck?! You whore! You're a whore! Oh my god!" Paul screamed as he paced around the campsite, his arms spread wide and his palms up, as if he didn't understand why she had done what she had.

I was frozen in place. I didn't know what to say or if I even had anything to say. Besides, I was sure he didn't want to hear from me. So I just watched and listened to Paul rant—a very well-deserved rant, to be fair. I felt bad.

Robin didn't say much either, other than a weak, "Nothing happened. Please calm down," which was completely unbelievable.

Paul then climbed into the back of his truck, continued to scream, and started throwing bins of supplies all over the campsite. By this point, his vocabulary appeared to have been reduced to just two words: "fuck" and "whore."

After he was done angrily tossing all of the supplies from his truck, he sped off with Gus the dog, leaving us alone at the campsite.

I walked over to Robin and wrapped my arms around her. "It'll be okay. We'll figure it all out," I said, really trying to convince myself more than Robin.

Without saying a word, Robin took my hand and led me back to the van.

CHAPTER 4

HIGH SCHOOL
DRUGS, FIGHTING, AND LAWYERING

In 1992, Tiger Woods became a PGA golfer, Pearl Jam was the hottest band, and I was about to start my high school career.

"I'm not feeling anything," I said, frustrated, passing the homemade tinfoil pipe back to Michael—a kid I'd thought was a Goody Two-shoes up until that point—who lived across the street from me.

"I think it takes a few times," he said before he inhaled.

It was clear neither of us knew what we were doing. The lights in the Saint Luke's Church parking lot were not shining brightly enough to expose our nefarious activities in the dark corner, where we sat propped up against a chain-link fence.

The first day of high school was less than two weeks away, and I was attempting to get high on weed for the first time. Sure, I'd gotten a buzz before; I'd swigged whatever liquor was in Triple B's stash or chugged a beer from my friends' parents' refrigerator or that someone swiped from the store. I was always up for a new buzz.

The summer before high school, a group of us spent almost every day at the local nature park that was an extension of the Cuyahoga River valley. We'd go rafting or just get lost in the woods exploring. To add to our adventure, someone always managed to get their hands on some Marlboro cigarettes or Skoal chewing tobacco. Most of us, being only fourteen or fifteen, couldn't purchase those items on our own, so we stole them from the store or "borrowed" them from our parents. Once I took a hit of a cigarette or placed a wad of chew in my mouth and got that buzz, I wanted more of it. And just for a moment, I was able to escape and not have to think about my home life—or anything else, for that matter.

Although Triple B's physical abuse was becoming less frequent as I got older, the emotional and verbal abuse was increasing. Triple B didn't shy away from calling me a loser or worthless. I was always looking for an escape, so my drug use just continued to spiral out of control.

Before the drugs, when I was in eighth grade, I actually had goals of being a good student and attending a private high school. I even spent a "day in the life" of a student at a few of the Catholic high schools in the area where I attended classes and shadowed a student. I liked the idea of learning, and I thought knowledge would give me the ability to achieve whatever I wanted and go wherever I wanted to go in life. I also thought that the high level of learning I craved could only be achieved at a private high school. However, private high school was not to be for me. I'm sure my mother would have loved for me to go to a Catholic school again, but our family just couldn't afford it. Plus, there were perfectly acceptable public schools in the area, and with my brother already attending public high school and my sister probably going to do the same, sending me to a Catholic high school wouldn't have been fair to them. I'm not even sure why my mom let me go visit those private schools in the first place; I'm sure she knew there was no chance I would be attending them.

I ended up at Cuyahoga Falls High School, which was only four blocks from my house. Notwithstanding my introduction to drugs the summer before, I tried, briefly, to be a good student. I even tried out, unsuccessfully, for the baseball team. I told myself that it was all politics—which, in some ways, it was—but deep down, I knew I wasn't good enough. I could have been better and practiced more and I could have refused to give up. But instead, I decided to move on. Although I ran track in middle school, I didn't even think about continuing in high school. It wouldn't have worked out anyway, because by the time track season came around, I was getting close to smoking half a pack of cigarettes a day. My goals of being a good student and playing sports were quickly eclipsed by three other things: drugs, girls, and my "friends."

I've never had a problem making friends. It's choosing the right friends that has always been my issue. The friends I had in high school were just an extension of how I felt about myself at the time. They represented what I thought friends were supposed to be. Constantly putting each other down and making fun of each other was how we communicated. Just like I didn't know what a father was supposed to act like, I didn't know what real friends were supposed to act like. This only compounded my rebelling and acting out. I had nobody I could confide in or to really support me. If I was anxious about a test, my friends called me a loser; if I liked a girl, they would tell her that I wasn't a good guy. I would have been better off asking a stranger for help or advice. They would ditch me to go to parties or take me with them to a party and then leave without telling me. In turn, I'd do the same to them. I continued to be friends with them because I didn't know any better and because I didn't think I had much of an option.

I had girlfriends in high school but wasn't sure how relationships worked, so girls came and went as often as the seasons changed. It was mainly my fault. If they got too emotionally close I knew it was time to move on because I was so afraid of feeling something and getting hurt.

Because of this lack of a support system, I wasn't the nicest guy. In fact, I was an asshole. Not just an asshole—I was a bully. Because my "friends" and I treated each other like crap, I treated the rest of the world like crap. I'd put everyone down every chance I got. I thought I was somehow superior to people who looked weird or had their own unique personality. I needed only the smallest reason to call people out. I had no idea what kind of impact I was having on others or how hurtful I was being. Inside I was just jealous because they seemed happy with who they were and weren't afraid to express it. I had no basis for any of the hurtful things I said to others. I just said them. It got to the point where I would pick fights with anyone—so long as I knew I could win. They didn't have to do anything to me; I just wanted to do something to them.

My drug use progressed quickly. I wanted the buzz, and all the "cool" kids were doing drugs—at least, that's what I thought the cool kids were doing. Whether it was huffing butane, smoking pot, or dropping acid, I wanted to do it. Although I was a regular weed smoker and beer drinker, the drug that I believe had the most severe consequences for me was the hallucinogen LSD—acid. At the time, acid came in doses, called "hits," on little pieces of paper about the size of a popcorn kernel. I took over two hundred hits of acid over the course of my illustrious high school career. As with most drugs, the first time I took it, I thought it was amazing. My friends and I would hang out at a local skateboarding spot, where we seemed to do drugs more than actually skate.

The euphoric feeling of doing acid was quite different from the buzz I got with weed or alcohol. It was like a whole new world had been opened up to me. I started noticing things I'd never noticed before: colors were brighter, people seemed happier, and I even thought I was happier, if only for a moment. It was like the blinders had been pulled from my eyes, and I could finally really see the world for the first time. I was now "awake" and looked at the world differently. I didn't really have any hallucinations—probably because we weren't getting the cream of the crop of acid in northeast Ohio—I just saw lots of trails of things that moved. If I waved my hand in front of my face, it was like watching a cartoon with the animation not quite sped all the way up, so there were trails behind it.

Although I thought I was getting a closer connection to the world and to my true self, I was actually going in the opposite direction. I was getting farther and farther from what I was seeking and what the world was actually like. And, as with any drug, the more acid I did, the more I needed to take to get the same feeling I'd had the first time.

Eventually, after taking acid too much, I had a "bad trip." A bad trip, obviously, is experiencing adverse effects from acid, and it can come up unexpectedly. At first, I was paranoid. That paranoia then grew into fear, which then turned into freaking out and becoming hysterical. I had a million thoughts racing through my mind at once, and all of them were bad. I thought people were out to get me, that I was going to die, or that I was going completely mad. While I was on this bad trip, I was certain I was going to be in this state forever. I thought I was going crazy, and I didn't know what to do. I begged the person I was with to take me to the hospital. That seemed like the only solution at the time. He refused, probably because he was tripping, too. The bad trip was one of the worst things I've ever felt or experienced in my life. I was so impacted by it that I vowed I would never do acid again—which was one of many lies I told myself.

Then, in a blink of an eye, freshman year was over. During my sophomore year, I decided to ditch my old friends and hang out with even worse ones. Luke the drug dealer seemed like the best option. He had long red hair, wore Alice in Chains and Primus T-shirts, and already had a reputation for being a druggie. Luke treated me like crap, but he also kept me high, so I took it. With Luke, I upped the ante and started doing cocaine. I don't even remember the first time I did coke, but I know I liked it a lot and always wanted more. And it didn't stop with cocaine. A few times, we put the crystallized form of cocaine—crack—on weed and smoked it. For some reason, that's where I decided to draw the line. I knew that getting into this realm of drug use was a whole other level and that I was going overboard and taking this drug thing a bit too far. I needed to stop hanging out with Luke.

Although Luke was not the best person to hang out with, he did leave me with a valuable skill: entrepreneurship, albeit in the form of selling drugs. The jobs I had as a teenager at McDonald's and Taco Bell weren't cutting it—not for a kid who needed to get high every day. The free food was great, but I knew it was possible to make so much more without flipping burgers or slinging tacos.

Thanks to my relationship with Luke, I knew who to go to in order to get larger quantities of drugs to distribute.

I started out small, just getting an ounce of weed at a time and breaking it up into eighths and quarters. I could buy an ounce of crap weed for around $160. I'd break that ounce up into eight separate bags, sell those bags for $30 each, and make $240. That's quite a profit margin. I often kept one of those bags for myself and sold the rest.

One ounce turned into two ounces, which turned into larger quantities of weed, which I could easily sell in a week. Going out to dinner with my friends became an odd experience because I would have over $500 cash on me, and my other friends were struggling to pay for their slice of pizza.

I quickly gained a name for myself in high school as the go-to drug dealer. This was essentially my life when I was sixteen.

Shockingly, my grades started to drop. It's not like they had far to fall in the first place. What frustrated me the most, though, was how everyone else my age seemed to be able to handle doing drugs and still function at a normal level, but I couldn't. It seemed like everyone was doing them, but I was the only one who couldn't handle their effects. Looking back, I see now just how close I was to the edge of the cliff, hanging on for dear life. I didn't realize that not everyone came from the same kind of home life I did.

When I wasn't selling drugs or getting into fights at school, I was at my friend's place becoming an expert in three things: doing drugs, card games, and playing foosball. My buddy's house was a safe place for all of us degenerates. I suppose it was at least better than running around on the streets. We didn't actually hang out in the house, but rather a remodeled garage behind the house that local bands practiced in. It was the perfect scenario: I was able to sell and do drugs as much as I wanted there. Plus, it was only a few miles from my house, so I had easy access to it. It didn't matter who was there—I didn't have to call beforehand—I would just show up and hang out with whoever was present. Somebody was always there and ready to get their buzz on. It was the perfect escape for a teenager.

At school, it seemed like I had a standing appointment with the principal every week because I was in her office so often. Her name was Ms. Peacock, and she was a short lady in her late forties who had a penchant for pastel pantsuits. Honestly, I don't think Ms. Peacock or anyone in the administration cared too much about my well-being. She never tried to help me or give me the tools to change. I was more of a nuisance she had to deal with. No one ever asked if my home life was okay or what was bothering me. I'm not sure if I would have told them anyhow, but I was never given the chance to find out. It was like I was a lost cause to them, and to be fair, I felt like a lost cause.

So often, I would be sitting in class, and a student would walk in with a blue slip of paper and hand it to the teacher. I knew exactly what that meant and so did everyone else: I was being summoned yet again for something I had done. And there was only one reason why I would be called to Ms. Peacock's office: I was getting suspended again. I was suspended at least a dozen times during my high school tenure, generally for getting into fights and for skipping school, the punishment for which was getting kicked out for a few days. It seemed like a great trade-off to me.

The worst part about suspensions though was that they called my mom; that's why I dreaded going to the principal's office so much. It ate me up inside knowing that my mom was going to get a call at work. I knew I was putting her through hell, and it made me feel terrible, but I also didn't do anything about it. I cared more about my friends, girls, and doing drugs.

Although I was constantly getting into fights, I hated fighting and was always scared. I did it because I wanted people to like me, to think that I was cool. I thought I had something to prove. I wanted people to think I was a badass fighter. I wasn't. Sometimes, my friends and I would beat up people together. We were cowards.

Eventually, the fighting got so bad that I was expelled from school. The fight that broke the camel's back was with a kid we called Buddy whom I was making fun of. I made fun of everyone because I thought that's what I was good at and people laughed, so I kept it up. Buddy wore a cowboy hat and had ripped-up jeans, and that was enough for me. At lunch one day, we got into a fight in the hallway. Because my druggie friends didn't care about getting suspended either, they jumped in to help. They knew I couldn't have taken him by myself. We ended up putting Buddy in the hospital. Not only did I get expelled from school, I was also arrested. I spent the rest of that year mowing lawns for a landscaping company and doing community service.

The fighting didn't stop just because I was out of school, though. One day, my friends and I were driving down the street, and we saw a few kids who we thought were different in some way, so we gave them the finger. To our surprise, they flipped us off right back. Little did they know that we had weapons with us in the form of a few collapsible batons, like the police carry. We parked our car and chased these kids down through various backyards and beat them up. We didn't use the batons on them, though. We didn't need to, as we had them outnumbered.

When we got back to the car, we were greeted by the police. It seemed a concerned neighbor had seen what we were doing and made a call. I got arrested, again, and charged with felonious assault. I was in major trouble. Not only was I facing a serious charge, but my mother had to hire a lawyer. Then we ended up getting sued by the parents of the kids. Luckily, the felony charge was dropped down to a simple assault, and I never went to juvenile detention. The other kids' parents got a small monetary compensation.

That wasn't the end of my fighting or getting arrested, though. I was arrested for trespassing, having an open container of alcohol in public, disorderly conduct, and disturbing the peace, all before I was eighteen. Then there were all the things I did when I got older.

As I was heading back to Cuyahoga Falls high school for a second shot at my junior year, I was starting to feel helpless. It seemed like I had nobody to turn to or confide in. To the school administration, I was just another nuisance they had to deal with. At the police station, I was just another juvenile delinquent to add to their statistics. I couldn't talk to my mom because she was so defensive about the father she had chosen for us that she couldn't see what was really going on and why I was acting out so much.

Luckily, a small miracle happened that year. I was still hanging out with the same kids, doing the same nonsense, but the school caught on that I didn't mind getting suspended, so they put me in in-school suspension, where

I had to spend the whole day just sitting in a room. I couldn't talk or sleep, and I was only allowed two bathroom breaks, which had to be supervised by a teacher and were at specific times. I had to bring in a bagged lunch, and my teachers sent my homework to me from my classes. Having to spend so much time in there was my saving grace, because I couldn't get into any trouble.

Mr. Brady was the in-school suspension teacher. I was in his room so much that he actually got to know me. He took the time to help me understand that I could achieve so much more if only I applied myself. He told me that I was smart and had a lot going for me. He was the first male authority figure to ever tell me that he believed in me and that I could be better. It blew my mind that not all adult men were miserable jerks that I needed to fear.

There was also Mr. Bishop, the biology teacher, who caught me smoking weed in the bathroom with my friends. He dragged me out of there, and I thought he was going to take me to the principal's office. Instead, something quite different happened.

"Kyle, the guys you're hanging around with don't care about you. They don't want the best for you. I promise you, when you have real friends in your life, you will figure it out right away because they will make you feel good about yourself," he said. I listened to him with my head down, leaning up against the wall, knowing in my heart he was speaking the truth.

These talks didn't instantly change who I was and who I was hanging around with, but they did plant a seed in my mind. Mr. Brady and Mr. Bishop made me look at who I was and what I wanted out of life. When I did that internal audit, I didn't like what I saw.

One day shortly after both of these talks and when I wasn't in in-school suspension anymore, I was sitting in my behavioral science class, staring out the window. Mr. Anderson was passing back a test we had taken the week before. Written at the top of mine was a large red "F." This wasn't surprising or unusual, but this time, I felt different about it. I knew I could have passed, and it really frustrated me. I felt as if I had no control over my life, and I felt it was time to make a change. I got up and left class immediately. I found my friend Brad, who I knew would leave with me, and asked him to drive me to drug rehab. I didn't know what else to do; I needed to stop the madness and chaos around me and I felt like this was my only option.

The rehab center I went to was for juveniles only, and it was in a fully functioning hospital in Barberton, Ohio—the very hospital my mother worked in. Once I arrived, I realized that I couldn't just turn myself in. As a minor, I needed to be admitted by court order or have a parent sign me in. I was actually their first patient to voluntarily enter rehab. They called my mom down, and understanding I needed help, she immediately signed me into drug rehab.

Drug rehabilitation was one of the most amazing experiences I've ever had. I felt so safe there. Nobody could hurt me, and I couldn't hurt myself by doing drugs. There was a strict schedule, which I liked. I knew when it was time to eat and what activities we were doing. I probably also liked it because I was with a bunch of other people my age who had also screwed up their lives. We would go to AA meetings, share our feelings, and see psychiatrists. I realized that I had a somewhat addictive personality and had difficulty doing things in moderation. I wasn't necessarily addicted to drugs, but I definitely had an unhealthy relationship with drugs and alcohol.

Triple B never came to see me, which I preferred. To him, my going to drug rehab was just more affirmation that I was a worthless loser. My mom did visit me, and she would bring me cigarettes. Thinking about it now, it was probably humiliating for her to go into a store to buy cigarettes for her teenage son in drug rehab.

The worst part of rehabilitation was telling my mom about all the drugs I'd done. We were supposed to tell the family members who visited us *everything* we had ever done as part of the healing process, but I was adamantly opposed to this. I was embarrassed and didn't want to hurt my mom any more than I already had. But they said it was necessary for my recovery, so I wrote it all down on a piece of paper and gave it to her. I could see the disappointment written all over her face as she read it. At least my being in rehab meant that she knew I was in a safe place and getting help.

After a month or so, I graduated to outpatient status. This was where I was supposed to stick with the program on the outside. It didn't last long though, maybe a few days at most. At one point, I headed over to the garage and someone handed me a forty-ounce bottle of Colt 45 Double Malt, which I immediately slammed. And just like that, I was back.

I was scared of not having any friends and of not being cool. I thought that if I wasn't doing drugs or hanging out with people who did them, I wouldn't be considered cool. People knew me because of the crazy things I did, like selling drugs, getting in fights, and running the trash can clan. "The trash can clan" was a nickname kids in school gave me and my group of friends because we congregated around a garbage receptacle, fittingly enough. In my mind, if I didn't have those things, I was insignificant. In fact, at one point, I actually told my rehab counselor that if I followed all their rules, I would be a loser. At seventeen, I couldn't comprehend how ridiculous my assessment actually was. I believed it so much that it scared the hell out of me. In high school—or at least when I was in high school—an outcast was the worst thing a kid could be.

Because of drug rehab, I had to repeat my junior year yet again. However, this time, I did calm down a little bit and eventually made it to my senior year.

Strangely, considering how much fighting I had done in my previous five years of high school, the most memorable and scary moment for me was when I was doing my best to avoid a fight. There was a kid a little bit older than me who didn't go to our high school but would hang out across the street from school, where all the kids smoked cigarettes when class let out. This was also where I could usually be found after school. Acting like my usual self, I often made fun of this kid to others, but my mistake was making fun of him to his girlfriend, who was in one of my classes. She told him about it, so after school that day, this kid was looking for me and as I walked past the crowds of smokers trying to find my friends, I heard a voice screaming: "Who is Kyle Robinson? Where is Kyle Robinson?"

I looked over and saw fury in the guy's eyes and saliva flying out of his mouth. The body attached to this raging kid had easily fifty pounds and six inches on me. I tried to keep my head down and walk past him as fast as I could; my heart was racing and I was scared shitless. However, everyone started pointing me out to him. I was fucked. Plus, my friends were nowhere to be found, so I was on my own. Making matters even worse, I wasn't a minor anymore, so if I got arrested, I'd be in serious trouble, and real jail was something I desperately wanted to avoid.

This kid spotted me and made his way toward me, ready to pound me into the ground. Me being the tough guy I am, I tried to run away from him, telling him I didn't want to fight. I ran around in circles trying to avoid him. A crowd gathered around us, and if someone had viewed it from a distance, they would have thought there was actually a fight going on. Eventually, a police officer came by, broke things up, and arrested us both without a punch being thrown. I was arrested for disorderly conduct, disturbing the peace, and assault and was facing jail time.

When my day in court came along, my mother accompanied me. I pled not guilty and represented myself because my mom wouldn't get me an attorney. I had explained to her that I hadn't done anything wrong, but I don't think she believed me. However, this time, I was telling the truth. Still, even though I had done nothing criminally wrong, I had caused the fight through my past behavior. No matter what she believed, though, my mom came with me to court. Triple B was absent.

The day of the trial, I sat at the defense table by myself, with my mom behind me. The prosecutor sat at the table to my left, the judge on the bench in front of us, and the arresting officer in the witness stand. The trial started, and the prosecutor started asking the officer questions. "Do you see the person who was involved in the altercation?"

"Yes," the officer said, pointing at me.

After the prosecutor asked a few more questions, the judge asked if I wanted to ask the officer any questions. *Hell yeah! This guy has no idea what happened*, I thought. I was so nervous and almost in tears as I tried to ask this police officer my questions. It was very intimidating, and I had no idea what I was doing. Still, I pushed ahead.

"Where were you when you first saw this altercation?" I said, my voice shaking.

"I was sitting in my police cruiser," the officer replied confidently.

"And how far away was your police cruiser from the disturbance?"

"About seventy-five yards."

"Was there a crowd of people around me and the other individual you arrested?"

"Yes, about one hundred or so kids."

"So you can say for certain that while you were sitting in your police cruiser seventy-five yards away, you could see clearly through a crowd of one hundred kids that I was involved in some sort of altercation?" I pushed back.

"Well, not exactly," he admitted.

"So you never actually saw me assault anyone?"

"No," he finally answered.

That was all the judge had to hear. The case was dismissed, and the charges were dropped.

That moment felt like one of the most amazing things I had ever done in my life up to that point. I don't believe the police officer was lying; I'm sure he really thought I was involved in a fight. And I wasn't truly innocent. I had made fun of someone who didn't deserve it and caused that situation. However, I was astonished at what I, as a nineteen-year-old, could do to defend himself against almost insurmountable odds. If I could do that, what else was I capable of? I had been able to stand up for myself, not only because the truth was on my side, but because Mr. Brady had planted a belief in my mind that I was smart. At some point, I had started to believe that and started to believe in myself.

By this time, I had a new principal named Ms. Allen. She was one of the better faculty members. She knew me well enough to know that I would get into trouble if I spent time going to regular classes. Therefore, she made sure I spent most of my senior year in in-school suspension again, which was probably the only reason I was able to graduate at all.

I finally graduated from high school after one freshman year, one sophomore year, three attempts at junior year, and one senior year. In addition, I had to take night classes and correspondence classes to catch up. It never even occurred to me to quit and just get my GED. I was going to graduate from high school; it was important to me to get my diploma.

I had wanted the experience of graduating high school so much, but my graduation ceremony itself was very bittersweet. My sister, who at first had been two grades below me, was a good student. She was graduating on time, which meant we graduated together. Her name comes before mine in the alphabet, so she got to cross the stage and graduate before me. This was supposed to be her day, not mine. I shouldn't have been there, taking her moment away from her. I can't imagine how that must have made her feel.

After barely graduating high school with a 1.04 GPA and a class rank of 376 out of 380, college was not on my mind at all.

CHAPTER 5
WASHINGTON STATE
WHEN YOU CAN'T BEAT 'EM, JOIN 'EM

I woke up, crawled to the back of the van, and opened the rear door. As I looked around, the previous night's debauchery hit me like a tidal wave. Beer bottles were strewn all over the site, stakes and dragons spilled out of the containers Paul had tossed from his truck, and a faint wisp of smoke still rose from the fire pit. Robin, hearing me open the van door, woke right after me. She didn't say much, just gathered her things and went straight to the bathroom. While she was gone, I cleaned out my van to make room for all the supplies that were now occupying the campsite and threw away all the trash. When Robin returned, she said she needed to find Paul and talk to him. Although he had a phone, he didn't often check it or even have it on. Plus, he might have been up on the mountain without reception, or he could have been anywhere really. I thought it was reasonable for her to see what was going on with Paul, considering what we had just put him through last night. Of course, a small part of me just wanted her to let it go.

After cleaning up the campsite and packing all the gear, we headed toward Mt. Adams Cafe to grab some breakfast, and Robin finally explained a little bit about the nature of her and Paul's relationship. Sitting across from me in the booth, she disclosed to me in a nonchalant way that they hadn't been close in months and that they were in the process of getting separated. I listened the best I could with a pounding headache, waiting to hear just the parts I wanted: about how she intended to be with only me. Those words never really came. She continued that she and Paul had an understanding that they would volunteer together for the race and then go their separate ways. Debbie was counting on them. As Robin was explaining—or more accurately, rationalizing—us sleeping together was okay, we looked out the window and saw Paul's red truck cruise by. Robin jumped out of her seat and took off after him, telling me she would text me as she rushed toward the door.

I finished my breakfast feeling confused about what I was going to do and how I felt. I went to my van to lie down and waited to hear from Robin, not knowing if I was heading back home or staying to help with the race. This was a decision I should have had enough confidence and strength to make for myself rather than leaving it up to Robin. I'd slept with her and that meant something to me, even if she was married. I didn't want to throw that away if there was a slim possibility of a relationship—whatever that might look like. After what Robin had told me about their relationship, I was able to convince myself that what we had done was okay. Obviously, Paul saw it another way.

Robin finally sent me a text and told me to meet her at HQ; we would be getting ready to go up the mountain to continue to course-mark. I asked her if she wanted me to leave, and she said no. Even after everything that had happened, they were in desperate need of my help; we still had dozens of miles of trail to mark, and I was one of the few people who was capable of doing it. I asked if she had spoken with Paul, and she said she had. He hadn't said much, but he'd agreed to stay and help out with the race even knowing I would be there too.

Begrudgingly, I went back to HQ, both because Robin asked me to and because I didn't actually want to leave. Plus, I felt bad and wanted to apologize to Paul for what had happened. I didn't want it to be weird between us, though I doubted that was possible. Paul had been nothing but kind to me and I didn't respect him by sleeping with his wife while he was a few yards away.

Arriving at HQ, I immediately saw Paul loading up his truck with supplies and walked over to him. "I'm really sorry about what happened," I said nervously, waiting for his reaction.

Paul, with bags under his eyes and wearing the same flannel shirt from the day before, replied, "Now I know what kind of person you are. Just stay away from me."

I tried to explain further, but he just walked away. I felt like shit, because I had done a shitty thing and he didn't deserve that. I didn't follow him or try to press the matter further.

Obviously, it was uncomfortable being around Paul, but I still felt like I belonged out there. Other volunteers and Debbie had shown up, and we were all busy organizing food and supplies. This time tomorrow, we would be marking the blast zone of Mount Saint Helens and beyond, and I tried to focus on the excitement of that.

After loading the supplies in everyone's vehicles, it was time to head to the campsite where we'd continue the course marking. I rode out there with another volunteer, Robby, who looked more like a UFC fighter than a trail runner. He towered well over six feet and sported a braided black beard that he secured with a rubber band. We followed behind Paul, who was riding with Robin. I left my van behind because it wasn't going to fare well on the remote roads and I would be sleeping in just my Walmart tent.

We traveled by way of unmarked ranger roads, which made the whole voyage a lot longer. Right before dusk, we arrived at a dead-end road that led directly into the blast zone of Mount Saint Helens. Waiting for us at a makeshift campsite were two other runners/volunteers, Justin and Patrick. They were a little older, both in their late forties or early fifties, and were standing by a fire drinking beer when we pulled up. It seemed they had been waiting for some time by the excitement of their voices and how much they were talking even before I stepped foot out of Robby's car.

I found a place to set up my tent far away from Paul, who stayed in the cab of his truck almost the entire night, understandably upset and pouting. That night, we made hundreds of dragons around the fire and figured out who would be course-marking the next day. It became clear that the only two people who were able to actually course-mark were Robin and myself. Justin and Patrick were running the race, and they didn't want to log that many miles beforehand. Robby was injured and couldn't really mark; plus, we needed him to shuttle us around. Debbie stayed in town to continue preparations. That left Paul, and there was no way he was going to mark with me. The plan was for Robin and me to start marking right from the blast zone where we were camped. Robby would meet us at our end point with supplies and our tents so we could continue to course-mark the next day. Paul, Justin, and Patrick would drive around and set up signs on the road and trailheads. Despite everything, I was excited that it would be just Robin and me the next day.

Surprisingly, I survived the night without Paul killing me in my sleep. In fact, the next morning, Paul seemed to be in a better mood. He actually acknowledged my presence and answered questions I was asking. Although they were one-word answers, it was better than the silent treatment I had been receiving. Before we left, I went toward the dead-end road just beyond our campsite and looked into the clearing ahead. Before me was Mount Saint Helens and the aftermath of its volcanic eruption. I was pumped, because Robin and I were about to venture into this blast zone, alone and on an adventure.

As we entered the blast zone with our packs stuffed full of course-marking gear, the scenery was like nothing I'd ever seen. At first, we were in a regular forest surrounded by green trees and foliage. Then before I knew it, we were exposed without shade and with the sun beating down on us, surrounded by gray rocks and ash from the 1980 volcanic eruption.

As we went along, I tried to open up to Robin about myself, but she was being a bit standoffish and cold. Her unsmiling face said it all: she wanted to focus on the task at hand. We did talk as we marked, but we never got into what had happened a few nights before.

I quickly realized that the other night's activities meant a lot more to me than they did her. Still, I saw this alone time as an opportunity to show her who I was and to let her know how amazing I was, and I tried to take full advantage of our time together. Plus, I wanted to know more about her. She seemed so smart, and I had never met a girl like her in my life. Girls in the Midwest didn't look like her, think like her, or even talk like her. She didn't care what anyone else thought and wasn't following the latest trend or fad. She wore a trucker hat and led me on adventures to the unknown daily. I was captivated.

Finally, I outright asked, "So was that just a one-and-done thing the other night?"

"I don't know. I don't really know you," she responded, not wanting to talk about it.

"We can change that."

Brushing me off, she said, "We have a lot more miles to mark. I hope we have enough dragons."

The day continued without Robin really opening up to me. Twenty or so miles later, we finished the day's marking and ended at the Johnston Ridge Observatory in the heart of the blast zone. We ran down the paved path to the parking lot, where Robby was waiting for us with a veggie burger for me, a hamburger for Robin, and our sleeping gear. By this time it had started raining, my knees hurt, and I was exhausted and happy to just be sitting.

The temperature was dropping and it would be getting dark soon, so we piled into Robby's car and took off to find a place to camp. Because of the weather and how dark it was, we pulled into the first parking lot we saw. The entrance had a sign that read, "No camping, no fires, no alcohol, and no firearms." Naturally this was the ideal place for us to stay for the night. We set up our tents behind Robby's car, as if a ranger couldn't see them there. We all cracked open some beers, I lit a fire using the wooden stakes from marking, and we all gathered around the fire in our canvas camping chairs.

"If only somebody had a gun, we would be in violation of all the rules here," I said jokingly.

Without missing a beat, Robby ran his fingers over his beard as if he were thinking, set down his beer, got out of his green camping chair, and headed toward his driver-side door. When he reappeared, he was holding a black nine-millimeter pistol.

Maybe it's normal for people out here in the middle of nowhere to carry a gun, I thought. Aloud, I said, "We are so fucked if a ranger pulls in here. We're breaking *all* the rules." Which was thrilling and scary at the same time.

"What the hell do you have that for?" Robin asked.

"Ya never know. I have a concealed-carry permit," Robby explained.

"Let's put that away," I said. I'm really not a fan of guns and get nervous when they are around. We were, essentially, in the middle of nowhere and I didn't know Robby that well, so I thought it would be best if guns were not part of that evening's activities. Robby put the gun back where he'd gotten it and we continued to drink and talk.

Luckily, a ranger didn't show up that night, and we all went to sleep in our separate tents. As I was getting in my tent, I kept looking over at Robin, whose tent was right next to mine, hoping she would look back at me and come sleep in my tent. She didn't. I crawled in and tried to get some shut-eye. It rained all night, and nobody slept very well. Still, we needed to be up early so we could leave before anyone showed up in the parking lot.

I woke up in a drenched sleeping bag, dragged myself out of my waterlogged tent, and was greeted by the sight of more rain and gray clouds. Doing another long trek on the trails was not appealing. We cleaned up the ashes from our fire and made our way to the start of the next course-marking section, a daunting distance of nineteen miles that stretched from Coldwater Lake to Norway Pass.

"I really don't want to do this," I said, knowing I was still going; I just wanted to complain.

"You don't have to go," Robin said to my surprise. "I'm fine on my own." She said it in a tone that suggested she didn't actually want me to go. I chalked it up to her being in a bad mood on account of the weather, but it still hurt because I wanted her to want me to go. It seemed like she really didn't have any feelings for me, or any feelings at all. Then I kept second-guessing myself, thinking maybe I was too sensitive—that's what I clung on to to make Robin's feelings and attitude toward me okay.

"I'm going," I told her as I stuffed dragons into my pack.

The course-marking started with a brutal six-mile narrow ascent. We hiked up snow-covered trails, past mountain goats, and gradually climbed to the summit of Mount Margaret. Although I was exhausted, I was energized by the scenery. Once we got high enough I was able to look down and see the crystal-blue water of Spirit Lake near the base of Mount Saint Helens. I could see thousands of pyrolyzed trees floating on the surface of the lake from the volcanic eruption. It was a sight to see. I kept telling myself how lucky I was to be able to experience all this and I truly did feel lucky—despite the drama surrounding me.

Somewhere along the trail, Robin and I started actually talking again and getting a real feel for each other. We were finally becoming friends, and she was opening up to me. As we ended our journey down into Norway Pass, we saw Robby's car in the trailhead parking lot and started screaming at the top of our lungs and running down the hill toward it. Both of us were excited to be done and to get some real food in our bellies.

As soon as we got to the parking lot, I lay down on the ground with a smile on my face, exhausted. For the most part, the course-marking was now done. We made our way back to Randle to meet up with Debbie and the rest of the volunteers at the race headquarters.

Before we left the mountain, Robin and I decided that we needed to test the temperature with Paul and see where he was emotionally before I joined back up with everybody. We hadn't seen or spoken with Paul since we left a few days ago from the campsite near the blast zone. I decided to go to a hotel, shower, and wait to hear back from Robin.

It was nice to have a roof over my head, and I was able to take a shower and do my laundry. Plus, Internet access meant I could do some work. I laid out my tent in the field in front of the hotel and let it dry out. Although I was around a TV for the first time in over a week, I had no desire to watch it. I didn't care what was going on in the world, and I didn't want to know.

I kept thinking about the past few days and what they meant. I needed to talk to someone about this, but I couldn't because I was spending all my time with Robin, and I couldn't talk to her in an objective, unbiased way. Also, everyone else we were around had no idea what had happened. I called a friend from Ohio and told him in vague terms what was going on. He suggested I leave immediately, which was sound advice.

Of course I should leave, I thought. *That's what any reasonable person would do.* I'd slept with Paul's wife, and he'd caught us. It wasn't fair to him that I was staying. Why would I stick around? I had even told Robin I would leave if it made life easier for her and if she wanted me to. But, selfishly, I didn't leave and she never asked me to.

A few hours later, I texted Robin.

Me: What's the word?

Robin: You're good to stay and help if you want. Paul is fine. Someone asked about how long you were staying and Paul said "the entire race." So if you want to stay, it seems chill.

Me: Do you want me to stay?

Robin: Yes.

Me: I should probably say something to him and apologize again.

Robin: No, don't say anything.

This text exchange wasn't exactly a ringing endorsement of the situation, especially since Robin was adamant about my not confronting Paul again, but it was enough to convince me to stay. Still, I abided by her wishes and didn't say anything further to Paul about the situation. Plus, I rationalized to myself that I should stay because they needed as much free labor as they could get.

I packed up, got in my van, and hesitantly drove toward race HQ with a pit in my stomach. As I got closer, I couldn't stop thinking, *What are you doing, Kyle? This is crazy. You should just leave.* But I didn't. Not only had Robin asked me to stay, I was also out here for an experience and an adventure. And I was definitely having both.

I pulled into the HQ parking lot and saw that there were even more volunteers now. Robin wasn't there. I parked my van, got out, took a deep breath, and walked over to Paul, who was organizing food and supplies for aid stations, not knowing what to expect.

"What do you need me to do?" I asked Paul.

Paul looked up at me and smiled. "Good to have you back. We're just organizing supplies for the different aid stations. Why don't you help Debbie and see what she needs?"

It was as if nothing had happened. I was back in the tribe and back in the inner circle. It was the oddest thing in the world. I was relieved, glad to be back and that the adventure was continuing. Robin texted me to ask if everything was okay, and I replied that it was. It was really nice of Paul to accept me back but it made me feel more like crap because it showed what a good person he was and how shitty I had been.

I walked over to Debbie who was in the shed, which was basically where the church stores it's extra furniture and supplies. The furniture and everything else was moved to the back to make room for the food and supplies designated for each aid station. There were thirteen separate piles—one for each aid station—and a sign on the wall indicating which station each pile was for. When the aid station captains came to pick up their supplies, we would have it all ready to go for them, thanks to a detailed checklist.

Aid stations at ultra-marathons are like buffets. There are choices of fruits: bananas, watermelon, oranges, grapes, and more. Runners can also get pretty much any sugary snack they desire: M&Ms, gummy bears, cookies, and granola bars. It's all there. There's also hot food, such as pancakes, tacos, grilled cheese, hamburgers, and soup. Fluids are abundant, too, and racers can get endless amounts of water, electrolyte-heavy sports drinks, running gels, all kinds of soda, coffee, and tea. There are heaters, coolers, ice, tents, and sleeping pads, all so the runners can stay full, hydrated, and well rested to complete the grueling race. Debbie's races were a top notch, first class operation and spared no expense making sure all participants had an experience of a lifetime.

Transporting all of these supplies, plus the gas, butane, and generators to run the aid station properly, can be a major challenge. The race would be going through some very remote parts of the Cascades, and we would need an all-wheel-drive vehicle to get to some of the destinations. To save on supplies, once an early aid station closes down, the volunteers pack it all up and move the supplies to a later aid station location.

I worked alongside other volunteers whom I would be spending the next several months with: Brian, Pam, Debbie, and Robby, who had been shuttling us around earlier. Brian was from Arizona, and he was tall with a shaved head. Debbie, whom we affectionately called "Auntie," because she seemed like a relative to us all based on how she was looking out for us, had dark hair and was from Washington State and was running the entire show. Pam was a military vet with short black hair; we called her "General."

Getting a trail name is a kind of rite of passage in this world. Mine was "Sheriff," on account of me being a lawyer. Robin was "Wilderness" or "Wild" because she seemed to know everything about the backcountry and mountains. Paul was "Hermit" because he liked to be alone. Robby was "Gunner" for obvious reasons. Once I received my trail name, it felt like I was truly part of the tribe. Everyone who had the honor of a trail name also had to wear a trucker hat at all times—every single one of us wore one. We were all from different parts of the country with different personalities but the trail brought us together.

We were also bound together by how dirty we were. We went days without showering, sometimes even weeks. We did have the option of a solar shower, but it sounds a lot warmer than it actually is. Basically, it's a plastic bag filled with water and left out in the sun to get warm. Once someone is ready to shower, they just prop the bag up on a hook, get underneath it, and clean as much dirt and odor off as they can. It can be difficult to prop the bag up because of its weight, and sometimes, they might have to sit down to shower because the bag hangs so low. A solar shower won't get someone as clean as a regular shower, but when someone smells terrible and they haven't showered for days on end, it's amazing how clean they can feel after one.

The day before the race began, all of the runners met in the church for a pre-race meeting. Debbie explained aid stations and how the race would go. Paul and I went over the course in mile-by-mile detail, explaining where the aid stations were, what the terrain was like, and where they might be able to find water if they ran out. This meeting was also where all of our course-marking became particularly valuable. We were able to give details on the exact state of the terrain from just days before they ran it.

The next day, the runners began their journey near the starting point for climbing Mount Saint Helens in the winter. Before the runners set off we equipped each of them with a GPS tracker.

Most runners had "crew," a group of people that would drive to each aid station, tend to their runner's specific needs, and bring specialty items that were not at the aid stations. Not every runner had a crew though, and in these cases, they were allowed to drop bags at certain aid stations in advance so that when they arrived at the station, their drop bag would already be there, waiting. These bags might include a change of shoes or clothes, extra batteries for their headlamp, or aspirin. Then there were pacers. These were runners who would join someone experiencing a tough or low point and keep them company during their race.

Once the runners took off, there wasn't much to do except hang around at HQ and wait to see if any aid stations needed more supplies. We had good communication apparatus: we all had two-way radios, which had about a mile or so of coverage. There were also ham radio operators at HQ and at each aid station, so we could keep in touch.

At one point, we received word that an aid station needed more water and food. Debbie was going to drive Paul's truck up, hauling the supplies, and I decided to keep her company. Debbie had been given her trail name "Auntie" for a good reason, and it wasn't just because she had three nieces of her own and was always looking out for us. She made sure everyone had what they needed and would dole out motherly advice, all while directing the race. She was also one of my closest friends on my adventure. After knowing her for a few days, I already felt like I could tell her anything.

It was a long drive up the mountain to the aid station, and we talked the whole way. As we drove, we passed carloads of people driving back down the mountain; they had been picking berries to sell in town. We talked about our lives and what was going on back home with each of us. I brought up the subject of Robin and Paul. I wanted to tell her the real story. Fortunately, Debbie knew Robin better than me, as Robin and Paul had volunteered at other races she had organized.

I tried to start the conversation as casually as possible. "So Robin's pretty cool," I said nonchalantly.

Debbie looked over at me as she was driving. I could see Mount Adams though the driver-side window beyond her trucker hat. "She's one of a kind, that's for sure," Debbie said with a smile. She usually wore a smile.

"So I need to tell you something. I need to tell someone because this is eating me up inside. I slept with Robin a few days ago," I said, feeling relieved that someone else who knew Robin had this information.

Debbie didn't seem surprised, but she did seem interested. I told her everything about what had happened between me and Robin and Paul. I needed to know what she thought about it all and thought she should be aware considering this happened at her race. Unfortunately, she didn't have much insight to share. She warned me not to get too attached and told me to be careful. Also, she felt bad for Paul, because he was a good guy. She reinforced what I already thought about Paul and it didn't make me feel too good.

I had already figured out most of what Debbie was telling me on my own, but having Debbie say it just made me want Robin even more. I'd have to prove to her that I was somebody special, unlike other guys. I guess I wanted something I wasn't allowed or couldn't have. My conversations with Debbie helped form a special bond between us, and it made me feel a little saner. I had somebody I could confide in.

Back at HQ while the race was going on, Robin and I would regularly sneak off for a make-out session at night, and Paul and I kept our distance from each other. We would talk when necessary, but we never spent any time together. I could tell he still wasn't happy with me. And it was wrong of me to keep this relationship going while

Paul was around. I just didn't know what I was doing and I rationalized that if Robin was okay with it, I should be.

We occasionally saw runners who had quit or heard stories about others who had gotten lost and gone off the trail but eventually found their way back on. Then we received word that the first runner was a few miles from the finish line. It was a big event to see the first-place finisher, and we all cheered. Runners started trickling in after that until the DL—Dead Last—runner came in. That seemed to be an even bigger event than the winner, because they needed to beat the final cutoff time, which built up a lot of drama, and all the other competitors were there to see them finish. This last runner made it by minutes, adding to our excitement.

After each racer finished, they got to sit down on a chair, and a personalized pizza was prepared for them from a portable stove. One of the first questions they were asked upon crossing the finish line was, "What do you want on your pizza?" It was best when we knew what kind of pie they wanted before they even finished. When they were a mile or so out, we would get their order, so that their fresh, pizza was ready and waiting for them.

The awards ceremony was the next day. Debbie handed out awards to the top finishers, and they also made up silly, fun awards. There were awards for best hallucination, an award for helping out another runner in a jam, the DL award, and so on. The volunteers also got special recognition, including course-marking awards: a piece of wood hand-carved in the form of a dragon with course-marking ribbons attached to it.

We spent that night drinking and celebrating with the runners. My insecure self was always watching Robin; I thought that if she was doing this with me, why not with others as well? Besides, she was beautiful, and we were out in the middle of nowhere. Of course other guys would want to be with her. Paul seemed to keep a somewhat watchful eye on her, too, though he was much more diligent about watching me.

The next day, we cleaned up. We had to be out of HQ by the end of the day. Even with seven people working, it took most of the day to clean and load up the trailer. Soon, everyone was leaving and saying their goodbyes. It was over.

There was another race out in Tahoe in two weeks that Debbie was organizing, and I wanted to be a part of it. Plus, Robin asked me to volunteer with her. It looked like the awkwardness was going to continue, because Paul would be there too. In fact, Robin and Paul lived near Tahoe together.

Before we left Washington, I asked Robin if she would like to camp another day with me there, and she agreed. Paul would be driving separately towing the large trailer of supplies for Debbie with his truck. Knowing I was going to stay another day and not wanting to tip Paul off, I pretended to leave Washington when everyone else did, but instead I headed toward Packwood to wait. Robin got ahold of me a few hours later, and we met at the Mt. Adams Cafe.

Before we drove off to where we would be camping for the night, things seemed to be getting a little out of hand, in that, when I pressed her, she refused to say whether she wanted to actually stay with me that night. She mentioned how she might circumnavigate Mount Hood the next week and make some other stops along the way to Tahoe and said I was welcome to come along. But then, she also said she might leave that night, even though we had already discussed spending that night together. This seemed to be just the way Robin was: she would pretend we didn't have plans and make her own. I could tag along if I wanted.

I made a stand though: "I'm not going to just follow you around wherever you want to go. We should stay together tonight as we planned and discussed." I said it with confidence and authority.

She agreed to stay.

We went up to the mountain to camp. We parked and decided to go for a run. During our run, we discussed our lives back home a little more and talked about our families. It was nice because it was a rare sober conversation between us, and I thought I was finally getting to know her a bit better. When we got to a clearing at the top of the mountain, we could see Mount Adams and the Three Sisters volcanic mountain peaks. I had no idea what the other mountain peaks in the distance were, but Robin knew, and she pointed them out and named them for me. She knew the Pacific Northwest like no one else and that was one of the reasons I was so attracted to her.

After our run, it was time to eat, drink, and be merry. I had been sure we would end up sleeping together again, but Robin wasn't giving off the vibe that she was interested in doing so. She wasn't cold toward me, but she didn't seem into it, either, so I didn't push the issue. We went to bed without so much as a good-night kiss and slept in our separate vehicles.

The next morning, we discussed our individual plans over coffee. She was going to go running at Mount Hood. She didn't ask me to join her again, and I didn't want to tag along. She seemed to be implying that she needed some alone time, so I played it off as my needing some alone time, too. I told her I was going to drive around and explore, not really knowing where I was going. We left camp with a hug but no kiss.

I followed her down the mountain in my van, kicking myself for not kissing her goodbye and not really knowing if I was going to see her again in Tahoe. Once we got close to the bottom of the mountain there was some construction work being done and we had to wait to proceed along the road. I took this opportunity to jump out of my van and go up to Robin to say goodbye again. She got out of her car, I kissed her this time, and she kissed me back. She put her hands in my pockets and smiled. It was amazing. When we could finally proceed on the road, I kissed her one last time and ran back to my van.

She texted me a few minutes later: *Do you miss me already?*

I did. But I texted her back: *Who is this?* Trying to be funny and at the same time trying to play it cool.

CHAPTER 6
COLLEGE
NEW FRIENDS, SAME OLD STORY

Congress was going through proceedings to impeach President Clinton, Google had just been founded, and I, a newly minted high school graduate, decided it was time for me to lend the advanced skills I had acquired in my previous six years to the workforce.

I knew almost nothing about cars. Strike that. I knew less than nothing about cars. My knowledge verged on having barely enough skill to drive them. Some would say I didn't even do that very well. I wasn't sure how they worked, and I sure as hell didn't know how to fix them. Therefore, it was fitting that I got a job at a ten-minute oil-change place, where I drained the oil and replaced the filter. I'd learned the craft at another quickie lube place during one of my high school expulsions. The pay was decent, and I was able to work forty hours a week or more if I wanted.

Customers would roll in through the garage doors guided by me or an inattentive mechanic wannabe. They'd ask me questions about their transmission or carburetor and I never had any idea what they were talking about. I'd just nod and offer a "Hmmmm" or "Interesting," so it seemed like I had a grasp of mechanic knowledge. My go-to line was, "It could be a number of things.

You know how they put computers in cars these days." That usually stopped the conversation. If they inquired further, I got the supervisor, who was more than happy to pretend he knew what he was talking about. Thankfully, most of the customers who brought their cars in didn't know much about them either.

It didn't take long for me to get bored changing oil on a daily basis. Drain the oil, replace the filter, and replace the old oil with new. Rinse and repeat. I needed something that challenged my mind, or at the very least was different. I wondered if what Mr. Brady and Mr. Bishop had said while I was in high school was true. Was I really capable of more? Did I think I deserved more?

One day, as I was working in "the pit" under a Ford Taurus, watching the black used oil leak from the car and down the drain, I felt my life heading in the same direction. I needed to experience something different and didn't want to spend the rest of my life changing northeast Ohio's oil. After my tenure in high school, I wasn't really sure if I had what it took to go to college, but suddenly, I was willing to find out. *But is going back to school even the answer to what I want to change?* I asked myself. *And could I even get into college?*

Society told me I should go to college if I wanted to be successful and happy, and I wanted to be both of those things. I was, suddenly, sure that if I could just graduate from college, my life would be perfect. I could get a well-paying job, find a nice girl, buy a home, and start a family, like a normal person. At least that's what I thought I wanted. Plus, I kind of wanted to prove to myself and everyone—at least those who thought my life wouldn't amount to much—I was capable of more. I just hoped I wouldn't get rejected because I was more concerned about what people would think of me if that happened, and I almost let that fear prevent me from even trying. But, finally, I threw caution to the wind and decided going to college was my next step.

The first step in the process of my exploring higher education was taking the ACT. Most high school graduates who were college bound had already done this and were actually attending college. In my sixth year of high school, I had been so busy focusing on actually getting that elusive diploma that I decided to forgo taking the ACT. But now I had to rectify that.

I didn't study at all; in fact, the night before the ACT, I decided the best thing to do was go out drinking with my buddies. I woke up the next morning to the sound of my alarm blaring on my nightstand. I slapped the button to shut it up. I had a pounding headache and I almost rolled over and went back to sleep. But something dragged me out of bed that morning. I picked up my dirty, cigarette-smelling clothes from the night before, threw them on, and stumbled to my car. Barely making it to the testing site on time, I took my seat, and a few hours later, it was all over. I left and forgot all about it, thinking my higher education was a hopeless cause. I went on with my life, changing oil and mostly forgetting about my desire to go to college.

Before I took the ACT, I had done some research and discovered that the University of Akron wasn't all that selective when accepting students—it sounded like my kind of school! I had applied and signed up to have my ACT scores sent there.

So when I received a letter with the University of Akron emblem on it weeks later, all of my thoughts and desires about going to college came rushing back. I tore the letter open.

"Dear Mr. Robinson, we are excited to inform you . . ." it began.

I didn't read the rest of the letter; I didn't have to. I was overjoyed. My life was about to change forever. I don't remember my exact ACT score, but I apparently did well enough to get accepted despite my abysmal high school GPA. To me, it felt like I had gotten into Harvard. I had a chance, an opportunity to improve my life, and I wasn't going to let it slip away. I had to prove to everyone, especially Triple B, that I had what it took to go to college. Hell, I had to prove it to myself. I quit the oil-change place shortly after that.

I was still living at home at the time and looking for a reason to get the hell out of there as soon as possible. I wanted to get away from Triple B, but I was also just ready to be on my own. I got that reason when I received my acceptance letter. I immediately moved into a place right off of the Akron campus with some guys who were also trying to make a go at college. I rarely went back home after I moved out, even though it was only a short drive away. I didn't like being there, and I wanted to feel like I was far enough away that I was really on my own.

It was an exciting time for me because the guys I lived with all wanted to do well, and we fed into that and supported each other. I majored in political science because it seemed like an easy track without an abundance of math and science courses, and I was mildly interested in the field. We had a map of the school on the wall where we marked all our classes with thumbtacks and we studied together almost nightly. We were setting ourselves up for success, and I was excited. I loved being in the college scene, loved the idea of being around so many people trying to become better and do better. Just being on a college campus gave me goosebumps, because there seemed to be so many possibilities.

Before classes even started, I had my sights set on a higher goal than just attending and graduating from the University of Akron. I considered Akron a stepping stone. I really wanted to attend Kent State University. It was a better school with a much better reputation than Akron. Also, it was farther away from my hometown and farther from all my old friends.

Given my precollege academic background, I knew I would have to do really well in my first semester in order to transfer to Kent. I decided to quit smoking weed, cut down on the drinking, and study my ass off. In doing so, I learned that if I actually paid attention in class and did the work, my grades would reflect that.

And it worked. I did really well. I did better than really well, in fact. I got straight A's and made the dean's list during my first semester of college. I had never done that well in high school, middle school, or even elementary school. After taking six years to graduate from high school, I was excelling in college. *I fucking knew it*, I thought. That report card was validation that I was capable of so much more. I was so happy to tell my mom and pretty much anyone else who would listen about what I had accomplished. My mom even put my report card up on the fridge at her home. I never heard from Triple B—not one word of congratulation. Nobody seemed as impressed as me though, but there wasn't Facebook at the time, so I couldn't announce to the whole world what I had done. Shortly after, I applied to Kent State, was accepted, and continued my political science studies.

Kent State is only twenty or so minutes from Akron, so I packed up my belongings and headed east. I got a job working as a carhop at a burger joint called Swensons, which was pretty much the premier job to have in college at the time. I'd run out to the cars, take their orders, and then bring out their food. On a good week, I could take home almost $1,000 in cash. Of course I just pissed that away, but in order to work at Swensons, I had to be in college and maintain a certain GPA—although both were loosely enforced.

Swensons was also where I met Don, my future roommate and the person who introduced me to my Kent State friends. He also introduced me to a fraternity, Sigma Phi Epsilon, or Sig Ep as it was known. I had never considered myself a fraternity kind of guy, but it was an easy way to meet people and get into the college scene. It was fun to go to formal dances and other activities with the sororities. I was even a houseboy for a few semesters, a position that involved making dinner for all the girls in a sorority house. It was a great way to get a free dinner and meet girls. Plus, our frat house had amazing parties that were exclusive to members and pledges. I was getting the full college experience, which is one of the reasons why I'd transferred to Kent in the first place.

I never officially joined the frat, because I didn't finish the rush process. I didn't want to pay the fees involved, and the kids I was rushing with were a lot younger than me; even the guys who were guiding me through were younger than I was and I had a hard time respecting the process. Even more importantly, I found another group of people that I related to more.

There were a bunch of guys who had either quit the frat or gotten kicked out, so it made sense for us all to get a house together right next to the frat house. The house was painted baby blue and it came to be known as the Blu House. There was a total of eight frat "rejects" in the house. These guys liked to drink and smoke, so I was soon back at it. Still, these were good guys, not like my friends in high school, and they supported me, cared about me, and took an actual interest in my life. But they just weren't good for me. They were at the drinking and drug-use level that I had been at in high school. I had already gone through that stage, and I was about to go through it again with them.

Girlfriends would come and go in college, where I still couldn't hold down a relationship. We had lavish parties—or as lavish as it can get in college—and we lived in a few different houses over the years. We managed to trash the Blu House so badly that the landlord sued us all for damages. Admittedly, it was really bad: doors were broken, the carpet was soaked with beer, and we never once cleaned the entire place.

All of this partying was fun at the time, but it took a toll on my grades. Unlike at the University of Akron, where I'd made the dean's list, at Kent State, I never came close. In fact, I was on academic probation for most of my time there. They actually tried to kick me out at one point, and I had to write a letter to the dean explaining why they should let me stay in school. I went to school all throughout the year, even during the summer. I knew deep down that if I took off even one semester, I wouldn't go back. I somehow managed to limp through to my senior year of college.

When I wasn't in class or working, I was drinking. The local college bars were only a few blocks from where we lived, but whenever we wanted to head down there, even if it was nice out, we usually drove. One early April afternoon in 2001, I decided to take my 1995 Jeep Wrangler down to the bar with three other people. We hit up Buffalo Wild Wings first and chugged some twenty-two-ounce Budweisers. Then it was on to Glory Days, where we drank many sugar-free Red Bull-and-vodkas—my drink of choice in college—as fast as we could. Finally, it was time to hit up Ray's Place, where we would spin their "shot wheel." This wheel was similar to the one on *Wheel of Fortune*, but instead of numbers, it had different liquors. We all took multiple turns on the wheel, taking down shots of Fireball, Jägermeister, and Jack Daniel's. We were getting slammed in the middle of the day for no reason; we just felt like it.

After four or so hours of heavy drinking, it started to get dark out, and we wanted to go home and change our clothes so we could go back out and drink some more with a different crowd. I decided the smart thing to do was for me to drive us back to our house. *It's only a few blocks away. What could go wrong?* I thought. I'd made this drive dozens of times before in worse condition.

We all piled into the Jeep, and I started blasting Oasis from the car's speakers. Everything was going well; we were all laughing and singing "Wonderwall." Until we weren't.

I took a left turn onto University Drive, where we lived now, from Main Street. Somehow, I hit the gas hard, and before I knew it, chaos had ensued. There was a sudden impact and the crashing sound of my Jeep's front end imploding.

After the impact, I looked around at everyone else in the Jeep and asked if they were okay. I didn't get much of a response. Two of my passengers simply jumped out and walked back to our place, which was only a half block away. I could see my house from the scene of the accident. Then I looked over at the person in the passenger seat; she seemed to be fine. I wasn't physically hurt at all besides a few scratches.

I tried to restart my Jeep and get the hell out of there, but it wouldn't move. By this time, I could hear the sirens of the ambulance, police, and fire department on their way. The passenger who had stayed in the Jeep with me got out and went over to the ambulance when it pulled up. *I hope she's okay*, I thought.

I exited the Jeep and walked around to the front to assess what had happened. The front was completely smashed in around a telephone pole, which was now leaning at a thirty-five-degree angle. As I had taken the turn, I had somehow accelerated the Jeep to almost forty miles per hour before crashing into the pole. As I stared at the carnage I had just created, I noticed that the blue-and-red lights from all the emergency vehicles were bouncing off the Jeep and the surrounding houses. They looked unusually bright, and it took me a moment to realize that was because when I took out the telephone pole, it had knocked out the electricity. I later learned the electricity outage had impacted a ten-block radius.

The next thing I noticed was two police officers headed straight toward me. "This your Jeep?" one of them asked as they approached.

"Yep," I quickly replied, feeling a bit dazed and knowing what was about to happen.

"And you were driving it?" the cop continued.

"Yep."

"How drunk are you?" the other officer finally asked. I guess they could tell by the smell on my breath and by how I was conducting myself. Not to mention the catastrophe behind me.

I turned around, looked at the Jeep, and then looked at the telephone pole. I faced the officers again and said, "Not drunk enough to cause this," pointing at my totaled Jeep. And I believed it.

"Turn around and put your hands on the hood," one of the officers commanded.

I complied, and they arrested me on the spot without even conducting a formal sobriety test. There was no need; I was clearly drunk. They placed me in the cop car with my hands cuffed behind my back. As I sat locked in the police cruiser, I saw the girl who had been sitting next to me in the Jeep go off in an ambulance and head to the hospital. I was growing concerned for her well-being. *God, I hope she's okay. I hope everyone is okay*, I thought.

As I watched the scene unfold from the backseat of the cop car, with more police and firemen showing up by the minute and the red-and-blue lights bouncing off of everyone and my totaled Jeep, I realized that my cell phone was still in my back pocket. They had searched me but didn't take my phone for some reason.

I managed to wriggle the early-2000s flip cell phone out of my pocket and throw it on the seat beside me. I leaned over and dialed the first person who came to my mind: my mom. I almost had to lie down on the seat to put my ear to the phone because I couldn't use my cuffed hands. "Mom, I need you to meet me at the Kent police station," I slurred over the phone.

"What's going on?" she asked, sounding like I had woken her up.

"There's been an accident. Please meet me there." And with that, I hung up.

I was transported to the police station and put in a holding cell. I kept inquiring about all the passengers in my Jeep and was told that everyone was at the hospital getting treated, even the two who had left the scene on foot. Eventually, I was released on my own recognizance and saw my sister and mom in the police station lobby in tears. I hadn't even needed to call my mom to be released. I'm still not sure why I did and put her through all this—probably because I was scared and didn't know what was going to happen.

I begged my mom to take me to the hospital so I could see my friends who had been in the Jeep with me. She tried to talk me out of it, but I insisted. As it turned out, she was probably right. I wasn't prepared for what was waiting for me at the hospital.

Everyone's parents and family members were there, attending to their respective kids, and they were not happy to see me. They were all staring me down; they wouldn't even talk to me. I apologized to everyone as best I could and left shortly after.

That night, I felt shame, embarrassment, and regret. *Maybe Triple B was right about me all along,* I thought. Thankfully, nobody was permanently injured, though I'm sure some of them have lasting effects from that night. I know I do.

I was charged with driving under the influence (DUI) and reckless operation of a vehicle. It could have been a lot worse, especially if someone had been seriously injured. This time I decided not to represent myself and hired a lawyer who specialized in college kids charged with DUIs. We went to court, and the prosecutor ended up offering to drop the reckless operation charge if I pled guilty to driving under the influence, which I did. I had to pay court costs and spend a weekend at an intervention program.

The intervention program took place at a local Holiday Inn, where I met with counselors and attended AA meetings. For the second time in my life, I was in some sort of drug rehab, and this time, it had been forced upon me. In order to get released from the program, I needed to talk about how my drinking was a problem and promise to not drink again; only then would they allow me to go on with my life. I said what they wanted to hear and promised not to drink, though I didn't keep that promise for very long. Although I didn't drink and drive again for some time—mostly because my license was suspended and I didn't have a car anymore—I basically picked up right where I left off.

Not much changed after my DUI. It should have been a big wake-up call, and it was. But only for a moment. I suppressed the memories and feelings it stirred up and pretended that it wasn't a big deal. A lot of kids get DUIs in college; I normalized what wasn't normal.

I immediately got back in the swing of things and partied every night. Instead of calming down with the drinking and drug use, I decided to ratchet it up. Tuesdays became our cocaine night, dubbed "tutting Tuesdays," where we would do coke all night until we ran out. I pulled all-nighters constantly, but it was never to study or get a paper done; it was to do coke. I made excuses for my drug use: everyone was doing it; I was in college now, so it was okay; at least I was trying to make something of myself. I also rationalized it because I wasn't selling drugs this time. Somehow, that made me a better person. It was almost like high school all over again, except I wasn't getting into as many fights, and I was now legally allowed to drink.

It was easy for me to get sucked into unhealthy patterns, mostly because I didn't have any healthy patterns. I was making bad decisions and then just kept making more of them. It was like a snowball effect. The bad decisions may not have been the easier route, but they seemed like an easier route for me. Plus, it was the route all my friends were taking.

Soon, I wanted to have the same feeling I'd had when I was selling drugs: having copious amounts of money and everyone wanting to get ahold of me and be around me. In reality, I just wanted to be wanted and feel significant. My solution was to start gambling. And not just regular gambling; no, I would be a bookie and take other people's bets. I focused on college and pro football, though during baseball playoffs I also took some bets. If there was a chance I'd make money, I'd take the bet.

Prior to this, I was familiar with how sports odds and spreads worked. I occasionally gambled on games and liked to watch sports. However, when I was making bets on my own, I usually lost and had to pay the bookie a lot of money. At one point, I thought to myself, *I should be the one taking bets*, so I did.

Being a bookie wasn't everything I thought it would be, though. I don't think I was very good at it, because I wasn't really making any money. I was even cheating the system at times by adjusting the spreads and the odds, but that just made matters worse. I'd either owe a lot of money or I'd have friends upset with me because they now owed me a lot of money. Also, I had no real way to force people to pay me back. Sometimes I'd get mad at friends if we were out and they were buying drinks even though they owed me money on a bet. It was an easy way to lose friends and make people not like me.

My only saving grace was that I was making decent money at Swensons. It was a shitty feeling working and picking up extra shifts just to pay back gambling debts.

Finally, after four years of college, I managed to graduate from Kent State University in August of 2003 with a Bachelor of Arts degree in political science with an impressive 2.02 GPA. The only reason I was able to graduate college at all was because I attended classes every day, save the day I got my DUI.

The day of the graduation ceremony, I drove to the arena where it would be held, parked my car, and pulled out a joint to celebrate. I got high by myself in my car before walking across the stage, so I don't remember most of it. I don't even know who the keynote speaker was or what they talked about.

That evening, my mom had a huge party at my house. We rented a tent and got a keg. I invited everyone I knew to show them what I had accomplished; I was proud. I invited my old high school principals and teachers, but none of them showed. I had managed to graduate from college before all of my high school friends. I thought it was quite an accomplishment.

With a college degree in hand, I was now ready to go out into the "real" workforce. However, I had a few problems: no job prospects, a dismal GPA, and no connections. Therefore, I got a job working construction with one of my friends, Chris, at his father's company.

This was a really low point in my life. We would get up every morning, get coffee, stop by the job site, do nothing, leave at ten a.m. to go to McDonald's or whatever fast-food joint was open and chow down, sleep in the truck, do an hour of work, and then go straight to the bar. This routine went on for the better part of a year, and I gained about fifty pounds. At one point, I was pushing the scale at over two hundred pounds. Not only was I fat; I was downright obese. I didn't feel good about myself or about my life. During this time, I was applying for "real" jobs but didn't have any "real" work experience, so nothing came along.

Then one day, my friend Brad, who was living in San Francisco at the time, gave me a call. His roommate was moving out, he now had an extra room, and he wanted to know if I wanted to move in. He didn't have to ask twice. I immediately agreed to go live in California. After all, what else was I going to do? California seemed like the ultimate escape. Not owning much of anything, I packed up a suitcase and made the lonely cross-country drive.

CHAPTER 7

LAKE TAHOE
NOTHING IS AS IT SEEMS

After I kissed Robin goodbye at the bottom of the mountain in Washington, I typed Cleveland, Ohio into my GPS. I had been gone a little over three weeks at this point, and I needed to check on my apartment and pick up the mail that had been piling up. Besides, I didn't really have anywhere else to go, and I needed to recuperate if Tahoe was going to be anything like Washington. Heck, at this point, I was fantasizing about sleeping in my own bed.

I had lied when I told Robin I was going to just drive around the Pacific Northwest, maybe going as far as Colorado. I didn't want to look like a crazy person going all the way back to Ohio when I was, possibly, going to be volunteering out at the race in Tahoe. Also, I didn't want her to think I didn't want to help out at the next race, giving her a reason to not ask me to come.

As I approached the Ohio state line and saw signs that read "Cleveland—101 Miles," I got a weird feeling. This feeling only intensified as I got closer to Ohio and farther away from the mountains. It was a feeling of dread over what was waiting for me there: my old self. Not that I was a new person. I was still me, unable to confront my past or the mistakes I had made or was making. Apparently, Ohio now represented a lot of the mistakes, shame, and trauma I carried within me. It had been so nice to be around different people with different mind-sets and different lifestyles. I didn't think too much about the incident with Paul or how it impacted him, or how big a train wreck I was. I was trying to block that out of my mind and focus on the possibilities of my future. Ohio was a very different world from the one I had just left behind, and I didn't want to face it. I took a deep breath and told myself I'd only be there for a week or so. On the bright side, being back in Ohio did give me some peace of mind, because I was able to focus on work for a bit. Plus, it was nice knowing that my apartment hadn't gone up in flames and I hadn't been robbed.

A few days after I arrived back, Robin sent an email to everyone who would be course-marking and volunteering in the early days before the race in Tahoe: "I'm forwarding you all the course-marking schedule. We will begin on Tuesday, at Race Headquarters and go about 26 long, hard, but really fun miles. You are welcome to come by whenever. Maybe getting everyone together that can by Monday night at my place?"

"My place"? As in, the place she lives with Paul? I thought, incredulous. *Paul is okay with this? He couldn't be. Who would be?*

Also in the email were some house rules and information about Gus and cleaning up, and warnings about bears breaking into our cars and the garage at night.

After spending a little over a week in Ohio focusing on work, I was able and ready to take another extended trip. I left once again, this time making the cross-country drive to Lake Tahoe. Before arriving, I stopped at REI in

Reno and finally purchased some real camping gear and supplies.

I arrived in Tahoe over Labor Day weekend, several days before Robin had asked everyone to be there. As I drove into Lake Tahoe, I passed Squaw Valley, where the legendary Western States hundred-miler starts. I got a chill just being in the area. The Western States 100 is the premier event in ultra-running. It's like the Super Bowl or the Daytona 500 for ultra-runners. I decided to spend these extra few days exploring the area and trails. The closest campsite I could find with vacancy was on the western side of Lake Tahoe—the William Kent Campground. It wasn't equipped with showers, but it did have potable water, a campfire ring in each campsite, and a place to park my van and relax. The campsite was a quick walk from the lake, and I took advantage of this fact by jumping in as soon as I arrived.

My early camping experiences had all been on the east side of the country. Before Washington, I had never camped in the middle of nowhere—it was always at a designated campsite. Because these campsites were near civilization, the closest I'd ever gotten to "real" wildlife was the occasional deer, raccoon, or squirrel. I'd been more likely to encounter a drunken neighbor who stumbled over from their campsite than a bear.

Camping in the western portion of the US at designated spots was a learning experience for me. Every designated campsite in the west has big metal containers with locks on the outside that are used as bear food storage bins. Not bins to store food for bears, but rather to store food so that bears won't eat it. I had to put all my food in these bins, even things like gum. If it has a smell, it has to go in there. I couldn't even leave it in my van, because bears could still smell it and were able to break into vehicles. I assume some campsites in the east probably have the same bear boxes—but none that I've frequented.

It was nice to be back in nature and in a new place I had yet to explore. Tahoe is obviously quite different from Washington and I went for a run on the Tahoe Rim Trail to check out the landscape. After the remote Cascade Range of Washington, where I might not run into anyone on the trails at all, Tahoe seemed strange, and I was initially unimpressed. I couldn't seem to escape the crowds of tourists enjoying the holiday weekend as I sped up the trail, constantly running into hikers and mountain bikers. However, I would soon learn that I was only scratching the surface of what Tahoe had to offer and that it had its own unique features, which I would soon fall in love with.

On my second day there, I met up with another volunteer, Brian, who had also been in Washington. It was nice to see another person from that race and to have someone else to explore the area with. Brian had never been to Tahoe before either, so he was just as eager as I was to see what it had to offer and was better at locating cool trails and areas to explore.

Brian was was comfortable with being outdoors and in nature, and he sometimes referred to me as "city boy." We went swimming and running on the trails and gambling at the casino together. We were basically just killing time, waiting for Robin to message us to come over. She knew we were both in town to help, and we were waiting on her instructions.

Robin finally reached out to us and told us we could come over early to stay at her place. However, her mother and her mother's husband were also there. Brian and I felt weird about showing up and interrupting family time, and

I felt doubly weird because Paul would be there, too. So we decided not to go over that night, and instead camped near her house in our vehicles. Later, I got a text from Robin that simply said, "Fuck You!"

I could only surmise she was upset that we didn't show up, and I knew she had been drinking by the way she was texting me. I tried to call her back and let her know we were close by and could come over if she really wanted us to, but she didn't answer.

We decided to head over to Robin's house the next day. I figured that they had gotten their family time in by now. Even though Robin's mom and stepfather were still there, we were assured it was okay to intrude. They had an extra room with bunk beds for Brian and me. I asked Robin if she needed us to bring anything, and she said alcohol—specifically tequila. I happily obliged; we stopped at the store and picked up tequila, and I made sure to grab a six-pack of Paul's favorite beer.

Their house was located west of Lake Valley on the south rim of Lake Tahoe and was situated in such a way that a set of rickety stairs on the side of the house led up to a back deck. Brian and I arrived late afternoon with the sun still shining. We ascended the stairs with bags of alcohol in our hands and were greeted by Paul, who was sitting on a red canvas folding chair on the back deck, drinking a beer. Before he was able to get a word out I immediately handed him the beer I had picked up for him; it was in my best interest to try to butter him up. "Thanks, man," Paul said with a smile.

"No problem," I replied. I wanted to say that was the least I could do—but thought better of it.

Also on the porch was an older gentleman with white hair and glasses. I assumed this was Robin's stepfather,

Sam. He was standing in front of the grill in Hawaiian shorts and a white polo shirt with a spatula in his hand and flipping burgers. After a few pleasantries, we proceeded inside through the sliding glass door, where Robin and her mom, Sophie, were.

Sophie was washing vegetables in the kitchen sink and she looked like an older version of Robin. She was short with silver hair that she wore in a braided ponytail. She had the same eyes, nose, and body type as Robin. While I was talking to her mom, Robin appeared from her room, wearing a black skirt with a gray tank—looking amazing.

"Thanks for inviting us over," I said with a smile, handing her the tequila. "Sorry about not coming over yesterday. We just didn't feel right about it."

"Not a problem. You're here now," Robin said cheerfully, taking the tequila and setting it on the table. "We'll have this later tonight."

"What was that text about last night?" I asked quietly, referring to the "fuck you" text she'd sent.

"Oh, nothing," she said, and quickly changed the topic. She was clearly pretending the whole thing had never happened.

That night, we all ate what Sam had grilled for dinner and enjoyed each other's company. After dinner, Robin grabbed the tequila and asked who wanted shots. At that point, Paul, Sam, and Sophie said good night and went to their rooms. Sophie and Sam were staying in the guest room right next to Brian's and mine downstairs. Robin and Paul had separate bedrooms upstairs, which was definitely odd for a married couple. I rationalized this as more evidence that they were indeed in the process of separating, so what Robin and I were doing was okay. Although

I believe part of it was because Robin was allergic to Gus, Paul's dog.

Only Brian, Robin, and I were left to do shots. As we all sat in the living room and the tequila started kicking in I texted Robin:

Me: I want you now.
Robin: How? Brian is still up.
Me: We'll figure it out.
Robin: Okay. I want you too.

Suddenly, Robin looked up at me from her phone, then looked at Brian and said with a laugh, "Kyle is bad news." Without waiting for a response, she continued, "Kyle, do you want a full tour of the downstairs?"

I selfishly agreed, and the two of us headed downstairs alone. We picked up right where we had left off in Washington: getting close while her husband slept just a few feet above us.

Robin didn't want to advertise what we were doing for a variety of reasons—her still being married the main one. For my part, I didn't care who knew. In my mind, they weren't really, truly married: there wasn't one aspect of their lives that would have made anyone think they were, besides the fact they'd told me and they lived together—which should have been enough for me not to pursue this relationship further.

Eventually, Robin and I managed to pull ourselves off each other and made it back upstairs. She wanted to go outside and smoke a cigarette. I was surprised considering all the running we did. It had been about ten years since my last cigarette, but Robin was smoking a little; she said it was because she was stressed out. I was drunk, so I took a few puffs myself, trying to make Robin think she was in good company. As if being myself wasn't good enough, I thought I had to smoke to try to win her over.

Brian came outside with us. Drunk from the tequila and buzzed from the cigarettes, Robin and I started making out in front of him. He didn't seem to care, and he never brought it up with me later. Now both he and Debbie knew about us—along with anyone Robin may have told.

After a while, we finished our cigarettes and all went inside. Robin and I went to bed in our separate rooms.

I woke up the next morning with a hangover and stinking like an ashtray. I walked upstairs to the kitchen, where Robin was already making coffee. "Good morning," I said cheerfully.

"Hey," she responded. Her body language was clearly telling me she didn't want to discuss the previous night. As usual, she was pretending that nothing had happened, and she started talking about the race and what we needed to get done.

Soon, Debbie and other volunteers would be showing up at her place, and we would be starting preparations in earnest. We would have to make new direction signs and a whole lot of dragons. Working at her house was a much more convenient setup than we'd had out in the woods; here, we had an actual home to work out of with the added benefits of bathrooms, showers, a kitchen, and civilization if we needed anything.

The next day, we started course-marking the trails of Tahoe. I was marking with Robin, while Paul led another team. It seemed to be a given that I would never go out on the trails with Paul again after the van incident in Washington. It was like an unspoken rule.

Once we got on the trails and away from Tahoe City and the tourists, my previous impressions about Tahoe quickly changed. It was warm enough that I was able to jump into half a dozen lakes, and I got the chance to run along the Rubicon and the Barrett Jeep Trails. As in Washington, we would camp wherever we ended up.

One day, our course-marking had us ending up at Loon Lake, west of Tahoe. We met up with Paul and his group of course-marking volunteers. It was still daylight when we all finished, and we were able to set up the tents that a volunteer had shuttled there earlier, along with additional supplies. It was the perfect end to a long day and a great location, except for one fact: the yellow jackets. They were swarming everywhere. Sure, we had noticed them on the trail as we went along, but we hadn't considered them to be much of a nuisance. Once we were at the campsite, however, it was as if we were standing in the middle of their nest. We couldn't do anything without being targeted by these weaponized insects. Forget about opening any food or drinks; they would be on it before anyone's mouth could get near it.

Suddenly, Robin screamed, *"Damn it!* I just got stung."

"Fuck, me too!" shouted Paul.

Not two minutes later, Brian and I were also victims of their stingers.

We had to be concerned because there would be an aid station near Loon Lake during the race, and if the yellow jackets were going to be this bad, we needed to address it. Informing Debbie of this potential issues, she had us get dozens of yellow jacket traps to hang at each aid station, which seemed to minimize their fury. Fortunately, yellow jackets go away once it's dark, and they stay away from the fire in general. Despite all of our best efforts, though, there would be reports of at least a dozen runners, volunteers, and crew members who got stung during the race.

Camping out in the middle of nowhere was one of my favorite things after course-marking for twenty or thirty miles a day. At night, I could clearly see billions of stars in the sky. When we didn't have cell reception, we were able to enjoy each other's company, talk, and drink. It made me feel like I didn't have a care in the world. We'd prepare food by the fire, play cards, and sometimes even set up a slackline for fun. We turned course-marking into a game, pitting Robin's team against Paul's to see who could get done first. This made it more exciting, because the losing team would have to buy dinner and drinks. It usually wasn't fair though, because both Robin and I were so competitive and would take it a bit too seriously, practically sprinting along the course, yelling at other volunteers to hurry up.

Some days, the trails in Tahoe were saturated with mountain bikers, and at one point, we even got caught in the middle of a mountain bike race. We had to step aside while dozens of bikes raced past us. It got so annoying that at one point, Robin, who was also an avid mountain biker, mumbled under her breath, "Fucking bikers." One biker heard this and stopped in her tracks and looked as if she wanted to punch us in the face. Luckily, we were heading the other way. We started running as fast as we could, laughing along the way. During all these moments on the trail I never wished or yearned to be somewhere else. That was one of the reasons why I stayed and put up with all the accompanying drama.

We ended up finishing course-marking early, which gave us some time to relax a bit before the race. Plus, we needed to do a little more aid-station prep, since Tahoe had more participants than the Washington race. On the bright side, it was a bit easier, because we had more volunteers than we'd had in Washington. By this point we'd left Robin's house and we were all strictly hanging out at headquarters—a campground on the west side of Lake Tahoe. Debbie was at race HQ while we were course-marking and she was getting supplies ready and had a few canopy tents set up. As in Washington, volunteers picked up their aid station supplies from us and headed out. Resupplying aid stations would be easier and a bit less stressful, because they were all easily accessible, unlike in Washington, and most aid stations had cell reception so they could just call in when they were short on supplies.

I spent a lot of my time before the race going from aid station to aid station, helping volunteers set up their tents or canopies or bringing supplies. It was an amazing way to see Tahoe. Not only was I able to run around the whole area on foot, I was able to drive around several times to see the landscape.

Finally, the race was under way and Robin, Debbie, and I were helping out at an aid station behind the Tunnel Creek Café on the east side of Lake Tahoe when we got the distress call about Tim being lost. I went to rescue him, not knowing what to expect.

It wasn't until I was about eleven miles in that I saw a figure stumbling down the trail. "Tim!" I screamed, and he replied in the affirmative that it was him. He was relieved that I had found him; I had never seen somebody so happy to see me in my life.

"Kyle? Kyle? Is that you? Oh thank god," he said, overcome with emotion.

"Are you done running away from me?" I said with a smile as I embraced him.

He had water with him, and he seemed to be able to move okay. In fact, he was in amazing spirits. He just kept thanking me. It warmed my heart and I couldn't stop smiling about the fact that I'd finally done something right on this adventure and I was actually needed.

Now the issue was getting him back safely. We were too far out to just turn around; it would be dark long before we got back. We needed to find an alternate route to a trailhead and to civilization. Luckily, we were still able to communicate with HQ, and they navigated us down the mountain and to another trailhead, where Larry, the medic, had been told to wait for us. To my surprise, Tim was coherent and able to move at a good pace and we made it down the mountain as the sun sank below the horizon and found Larry sitting on a boulder in the trailhead parking lot.

Toward the end of the race, snow hit the mountains, even though it was early September, and we started to get concerned for the runners, who were probably not prepared for this. It had been in the eighties during the day, but now it dropped well below freezing at night. Thankfully, there were no incidents.

Debbie gave me the responsibility of getting all the finishers' final times and photos so I could post them on the race Facebook page. It was tough getting the time of every runner who crossed the finish line, because they came in so far apart so it was hard to get any sleep. Robin was at the finish line with me. To make it easier, we pulled our vehicles up beside the finish and slept whenever we could. When we heard someone shout, *"Runner,"* Robin and I would jump out of our vehicles and make sure there was someone there to greet and congratulate them if Debbie wasn't there to do it herself. Imagine coming to the end of a race at three thirty in the morning with nobody there to see it. We had chairs and tables set up with food, water, heaters, and blankets for the runners. And, just like in Washington, they also got their own personalized pizzas.

One of the worst parts about volunteering was going to an aid station after it had closed down and making sure everything had been cleaned up properly. Aid station captains were supposed to ensure that the stations were cleaned up, which included taking all garbage to the proper receptacles. Most aid stations didn't have dumpsters, so trash would have to be taken away in a volunteer's car, sometimes for quite a distance, to throw it out. Some aid stations left their garbage because it "wouldn't fit in their car." This seemed to be an issue with many aid stations, so I was often responsible for picking up the garbage left behind. Once I picked up my first such bag, I understood why it "wouldn't fit in their car": the smelly, sometimes leaking bags were an assault on the senses.

The day after the race, we had a party with kegs and liquor at race HQ. There was a dining hall with an upstairs area with a kitchen and a dining space that we were allowed to hang out in. All the runners showed up, and there was an award ceremony. It was good to get everyone together to talk about their experiences—not just the runners, but also their families, the crew, and the volunteers who'd experienced their triumph as well. People were laughing and crying, and everyone was having a good time.

Later that night things started to get crazy. Most of the volunteers were drinking heavily and I had had my fair share of beer. I could tell many of them didn't drink very often, because there were people throwing up, getting naked, and acting ridiculous.

At one point during the night, as I sat on the floor talking with Brian and Debbie, I was facing the dining area, where everyone was mingling around tables. I could see Robin, who was facing me, sitting at a table between Paul and some other guy. Robin was smiling, and when I looked down underneath the table Robin was rubbing the other guy's leg, while she was sitting right next to Paul. Paul was completely oblivious to what was going on. She has been drinking a lot that night and seemed drunk. I was not happy and felt sick to my stomach. But to be truthful, I was not all that surprised.

While I was witnessing this, getting more enraged, I tried to make eye contact with her, but she wouldn't look my way. She wasn't trying to avoid me; she was clearly oblivious to what was going on around her, as was everyone else besides me. Finally, I jumped up and went over to her. I leaned in close to her ear and told her I was leaving for good. And I really thought I was going to leave. With that, I walked out of the dining area and down the stairs. Robin quickly followed me outside.

"Kyle! Kyle! Stop, what's going on? Why are you leaving?" Robin said, stumbling after me.

"What the fuck is wrong with you?" I screamed at her, turning around in the parking lot.

"I don't know what you're talking about," Robin said, slurring her words.

"I saw what you were doing," I said, still screaming.

"What are you talking about? Nothing was going on."

"I'm fucking leaving. I'm sick of this shit."

"Please, please don't go. I'm sorry. I want to be with you. I do." She was pleading now.

I was wary. She had been drinking, and I knew drunk Robin was very different from sober Robin. "Listen, I really like you, and I care about you, but you need to make some decisions about what you want," I said.

At this point I was trying to rationalize to myself what she was doing, as if it was okay and something I could forget about. I was drunk. I wanted to get beyond this for some reason and I clung to the fact that I thought she saw me differently to other guys and we had a special relationship—probably because that's what I'd craved my entire life.

She agreed with what I was saying, and suddenly, we were kissing.

I tried to get her to leave the party with me so we could be alone, but as we were talking, Paul showed up, and then it was the three of us in the parking lot of the HQ campground while everyone else was inside partying. Paul had been drinking heavily that night, too. He was staring at me but asked her what was going on.

Robin didn't want to deal with any of this drama, so she just got in her car and sped away, I assumed to go sleep somewhere. I tried to talk to Paul and explain to him I wasn't the one he had to worry about—though in truth, I was. He didn't listen to me and just went back into the party.

At this point, Debbie was coming outside passing a mumbling Paul going up the stairs. Sensing something was wrong she came over to me and could tell I was visibly shaken, and drunk. I explained the entire situation and told her that I wanted to leave. Being "Auntie," she convinced me not to drive drunk and to just go to my van and get some sleep.

I crawled into my van and I was on the verge of tears; angry about getting myself in this situation, and feeling worthless and sad, and not knowing how to fix all this—as if this were something I could fix. I knew Robin's actions were reinforcing the fact that she didn't really care for me. I was crushed to have what I'd known at the bottom of my heart confirmed.

I woke up the next morning feeling like shit. I hadn't brushed my teeth before bed, and my mouth tasted like crap. As I got up, I noticed Robin's car in the parking lot. *That's odd*, I thought. *She must have come back at some point last night.* I wondered if she had come back to the party and hooked up with that dude she was sitting next to.

I grabbed my water bottle and headed toward the bathroom to fill it up. As I was walking across the parking lot, I saw Paul running down the stairs from HQ toward Robin's car. I thought, *Here we go, what does he want now?* Not noticing me at first, he ran over to Robin's car and started screaming at her to get up and banging on her car windows. For a moment, I was worried he would break a window. For the few souls outside at this hour, it was quite the scene.

As I watched this play out, I assumed that the dude who she had been grabbing at the party was in her car with her. Paul probably assumed I was in there with her. I decided to get my water and then immediately drive back east. I was done.

Paul was screaming that there was puke all over race HQ. He was furious. Robin eventually exited her car, alone.

As I was walking past them to get my water, Paul ran up to me and shoved me. "What the fuck are you still here for?" he screamed. Getting closer to my face, he continued, "I knew you were going to be a problem since day one."

"Get out of my face," I told him, my heart starting to race. "If Robin wants me to leave, she can tell me so herself."

As this was going on, Robin was watching from her car. Paul's nose was almost touching mine by this point. He shoved me again, but I stood firm, saying that I wouldn't leave unless Robin wanted me to. He shoved me a third time.

"You don't want to fuck with me," I said. "I'm warning you." I could smell the alcohol on his breath, and I knew he really didn't want to fight because he had a bad wrist from falling on the trails earlier in the week. Eventually, he backed off, got in his truck, and peeled away. I was relieved not to have to fight him, but also that he'd finally left.

By this point, a small crowd had gathered to witness the drama. Robin walked over to me and asked me what had happened, as if she hadn't been standing ten feet away the whole time. I didn't say much. Besides, she seemed more concerned about the puke in HQ Paul had been referring to. She went inside to assess the situation with Debbie, while I went to brush my teeth and figure out what I was going to do now.

In hindsight, I should have left. It had been obvious to me before, but I just kept pretending. Every time I asked Robin if she wanted me to stay, it was an emphatic yes. So I stayed.

Most of the runners left that morning, but there was still a lot of cleanup to do. I told myself I would stay to help clean up, then leave. I didn't ask about the puke or shit and I didn't want to know. We also needed to pack up the trailer with all the supplies, which was a daunting task in itself. By this point, all of the volunteers knew that there was something going on between Robin and me.

Robin pulled me aside later, and we had a heart-to-heart. "I just want to let you know that I'm sorry for what happened," she began. "Not only about last night, but about everything with regard to you and Paul. I really like you, and I'm glad you're staying. It's completely over between me and Paul."

She was saying exactly what I wanted to hear to rationalize staying in this toxic relationship. It made it easier for me to pretend. Even though I'd heard this story before, I wanted to believe it this time. I knew I was just staying because I didn't want to be alone anymore, and I thought anything was better than that.

As we were cleaning up and packing the trailer, we decided to take a break, go eat, and finish the next morning. Debbie wanted to take all the remaining volunteers out for dinner and drinks. Robin and I rode to the restaurant together and sat next to each other once there. People were asking us if we were a couple. We didn't say a word, just smiled. It felt odd to be so open after hiding for so long.

The next morning, we finished packing up the trailer. We also had the opportunity to go through the drop bags that had been left behind. It was a stated and known policy that whatever wasn't claimed before the runners left was fair game for the volunteers. People left running poles, shoes, jackets, phones, and food. I was surprised by how many people left expensive race gear behind. We went through whatever hadn't been claimed and took what we wanted. The rest, we either donated or trashed.

Now that the race was over, I needed to decide what I was going to do next. Should I go back to Ohio or stick around in Tahoe? Robin and I decided we would discuss this over breakfast the following day. Robin said she wanted me to stay, but she also needed to see what the situation was with Paul, which was understandable, since they lived together. We agreed to meet up again in a day or two and go from there. So I stayed in Tahoe a few more days waiting on Robin. I got a hotel room near the casinos, did my laundry, and enjoyed having a shower and a proper bed.

As promised, a few days later, we met up and went for a run together at Lake Aloha, south of Tahoe. We ran for several miles and talked about the situation. As it turned out, nothing had really changed. It was the same old story: she needed to figure out what was going on with Paul. She explained that it would be difficult for me to stay and help out with races she would be volunteering at, considering that Paul never wanted to see me again and he would be volunteering at all the races too.

After our run, we said our goodbyes, and I assumed it was the last time I would ever see her. She assured me that we would, in fact, see each other again. She asked where I was going, and I told her I had to go back to Ohio to wrap up some business. I said I might drive around the west after that. She was planning to go out to Moab, Utah, the following month and asked if I wanted to check out some trails with her. I told her I did. We kissed goodbye, and I drove off to the east.

CHAPTER 8
SAN FRANCISCO TO LAW SCHOOL
WHEREVER I GO, THERE I AM

In 2004 *National Treasure* starring Nicolas Cage was number one at the box office and living anywhere but Ohio was my number one priority. I was on my way to San Francisco, California. I made the trip alone in a run-down 1995 black four-door Volkswagen Jetta that I had been able to purchase with the insurance money I got from totaling my Jeep in college. The Jetta, like me, was a bit of a mess. The transmission was about to go, the engine constantly overheated, and there were several electrical problems, including the windshield wipers not working. I couldn't fix any of these mechanical issues, but if the car needed an oil change or washer fluid, I was on top of it. I was concerned that it might not make it all the way to California, but I didn't really have any other options. I needed to get out there quickly because rent was due, and I was already a few days late. Still, the opportunity to live in California felt like a new start for me, and I was hoping to leave my past behind.

Driving that distance alone for the first time wasn't as enjoyable as I thought it would be. In fact, it was a complete nightmare. Because I was in such a rush to get out there, I had to sacrifice sleep for driving. A little over halfway through my trip, I pulled over and took a brief forty-five-minute "nap" at a rest stop somewhere in Nebraska on Interstate 80. The break was more to give my eyes a chance to rest from all the windshield time than anything. Unfortunately, I wasn't able to fall asleep because I was so uncomfortable from not being able to lie down. Plus, I was parked in a noisy rest area in the middle of the day. *If only I'd had a van I could sleep in.*

After my failed attempt at a nap, I decided to get back on the road, chugging as much Red Bull and coffee as I could get down my throat along the way.

There were times when the radio couldn't pick up a signal and just played static, and I had nobody to talk to. The silence bothered me, so I resorted to talking to myself. To pass the time, I played solitaire on the laptop that was open on my passenger seat. I had my right hand on my laptop, while I steered with my left. My left hand also held a Camel menthol light cigarette, which I was chain-smoking. Somewhere in Utah, I picked up my cell phone and noticed it was dead. I didn't have a car charger. I was navigating via printed-out pages of directions from MapQuest, and I got lost several times in Nevada. This was before everyone had GPS. I was going out of my mind from boredom, and I would have rather had my worst enemy sitting next to me to share the empty silence.

To add insult to injury, it started raining in Wyoming. I thought I might still be able to drive without the wipers because I had applied a rain repellent to the windshield, but the police thought otherwise. As I was driving along in the pouring rain, I looked out my rearview mirror and saw the blue-and-red flashing lights I was so familiar with. I immediately panicked and tried to remember if I had any drugs in the car. It was an automatic reaction. Luckily, I didn't have anything illegal. Then for a brief moment, I had to ask myself if I was sober. Yes, I was sober, but exhausted.

The cop directed me to pull over to the side of the road until the rain stopped, thus prolonging my trip more. I explained to him that I needed to get out to California in a hurry to pay my rent. He didn't care. "Would you rather arrive dead or late?" he said as he handed me a ticket. As though those were my only two options. He also mumbled something about my safety and the safety of others on the road. The rain finally subsided twenty minutes later and I was on my way again.

After fifty or so hours on the road, I was welcomed to San Francisco via the Bay Bridge. I drove through the small tunnel that led to the bridge and held my breath until I saw San Francisco's skyline slowly come into view. To my right was the pyramid top of the Transamerica building; below me was the Port of San Francisco sign welcoming me; and ahead, off in the distance, settled on a hill between Twin Peaks and Mount Sutro, was the Sutro Tower and my new future—my adrenaline started pumping. I was overwhelmed and relieved that I was finally here. Crossing that bridge was like crossing over into a new life for me. I had finally arrived; tired, overweight, and a bit delirious, but there.

Although the drive had been miserable, I had never second-guessed my choice to go out to California. There was nothing for me in Ohio but bad news and regret, and I was far more excited about the possibilities that awaited me here.

I made my way into the city and drove toward my new home, navigating the steep hills with palm trees lining the roads. Driving under the speed limit, I tried to soak in the sun and my new surroundings. In addition to Brad, I'd be living with another roommate, Mary, who was a friend of Brad's. We'd be living in a good area, Noe Valley, in the heart of San Francisco. The nickname for their neighborhood was "Stroller Valley" on account of all the yuppies and their kids living there.

As soon as I arrived at my new place I was forced to wait even longer to start my new life as I drove around the block several times looking for a parking spot. Finally, I spotted a car leaving and made my move. I parked and dragged myself up toward the four-unit house with dark-brown wooden shingles and a red roof and pressed the doorbell. Brad came down and opened up the gate. I didn't say much, I just handed him my rent check and asked where my room was. Taking my suitcase, he led me to my new empty room with a view of the house next to us. I could literally open the window and touch the exposed red bricks of our neighbor's home. Not having much to unpack, I went to sleep on the floor for fifteen hours straight. All I owned was my car, a suitcase of clothes, my computer, and my cell phone. When I woke up, it was time to start my life in a new city where nobody knew me. The only problem was that I'd brought myself with me. The first thing I did as a new citizen of San Francisco was head to Zeitgeist, a bar in the Mission District with an outdoor patio littered with picnic tables. We ordered pitchers of beer and drank the day away to celebrate my arrival.

The next morning, I woke up on the floor of my empty room hungover. I was broke and needed to get a job AS-AP. Not only did I have to start paying rent monthly, my college loans were coming due, and it looked like I was going to keep up my old lifestyle of partying. It seemed that I had put myself in a corner. If I didn't find a job, I wasn't going to be able to live out here too long. The next step would be living on the streets or living in my Jetta. I couldn't go back home, and I had nowhere else to go. At least if I was going to be homeless, San Francisco was the place to do it. With a fairly mild temperature and the ocean nearby, it could have been worse.

In truth, the rampant homelessness in San Francisco was quite a shock to me when I first arrived. On every block, there seemed to be at least one homeless person with a sign asking for help. It was more prevalent in Haight-Ashbury and downtown, but Noe Valley still had its share. But as with anything else, I got used to it.

At the time, the hotel unions were striking, and I was happy to take advantage of the situation and cross the picket line to become a scab. I went downtown to the best hotel in San Francisco—the Four Seasons—applied, and was hired the next day as a bellhop. This wasn't exactly what I'd gone to college for, but I was grateful to have an income. Plus, I knew the job would last only as long as the strike did.

Every day, I had to cross the picket line to go to work. The dozens of striking union members shouted, "Scab! Scab!" at me as I walked into the hotel. It wasn't the most positive or uplifting way to start my day, but I didn't let it get to me too much—I had a paycheck. Besides, pretty much everything was a new experience to me so I took it all in stride.

Being a bellhop was easy and interesting. The hotel served breakfast to all employees every morning for free, and during the day, all I had to do was bring people's bags up to their room—that's it. They'd tip me for it, too. Not only was I getting a paycheck, I was getting a free breakfast and leaving with cash in my hand from tips. I had to wear the stereotypical bellhop uniform with the black hat that looked like something a chauffeur would wear and a dark-gray coat with dozens of gold buttons sewed to the front, but it was a small price to pay for having an income.

I didn't understand at the time why the union workers would even want to strike; it seemed to me that they had it pretty good, what with the free breakfast and tips, and I was happy for their strike to provide me with an opportunity. I see now I was only doing the job for several weeks, and I wasn't depending on the income to support a family. If I'd had to keep doing it for a living, I could certainly have understood their asking for better wages.

While I was working as a bellhop, I was also trying to find a more permanent job before the strike ended. I knew I could find a server job fairly easily and eventually, I got a job as a waiter at Tony Roma's rib joint in Embarcadero Center downtown.

Embarcadero was a multilevel shopping center spanning four blocks right by the water, which attracted a lot of tourists. The waiter job soon turned into a bartending gig, which meant I was making even more money. I apparently moved up so quickly because I had impressed management by actually showing up on time and not calling in sick. I guess being on time was a rarity in California. In fact, everybody there was on "California time," which meant showing up ten or fifteen minutes late. Having grown up in the Midwest, I subscribed to the philosophy of "To be early is to be on time, to be on time is to be late, and to be late is unacceptable."

I was actually making really good money bartending. At the time, the minimum wage in San Francisco was $10 an hour, and in addition to the hourly rate, I was making tips. This meant that I was able to pay my rent, start paying back my student loans, and even save a little money. This was the first time I had ever been able to get my financial situation at least somewhat in order. Before that, my credit score had been in the tank because I'd defaulted on my student loans and cosigned for some of my friends' cell phones, which they'd never paid for.

I could have continued being a bartender and living in San Francisco forever. I had money in my pocket and little stress. I really enjoyed the San Francisco lifestyle. I ended up selling my Jetta because parking was a nightmare, and I didn't need it because the mass transit was amazingly reliable.

Days started melting into one another and I was getting into a groove. However, I always had this nagging fear in the back of my mind that I would wake up one day, forty years old, and still be a bartender. That wasn't something I wanted for my life, and I tried to snap myself out of the routine I was so getting used to. It was the same feeling I'd had when I wanted to leave the oil-change place. *There has to be something more for me.* While my living situation was great for the time being, it didn't really lend itself to personal growth. Although I was relatively happy, I wasn't living up to my full potential, which is what I aspired to do.

The only thing that was growing in my apartment was pot. My roommates liked to grow weed, so I got back into smoking weed again. I was pretty much in a constant daze, and I'd had enough. I knew myself, and I needed a change. In my mind, I still hadn't proved to myself and to all my haters that I was good enough. I still didn't feel like a success. Of course, it was hard to feel like a success when I was bartending during the day and getting high and drunk at night several times a week.

What could I do to make myself happy and feel like a success and make others think I'm a success too? My focus was on what other people thought about me, which was misplaced. But I didn't know any better at the time. I thought the answer was to make a lot of money. *What profession could I pursue that makes a lot of money?* The answer came easily: law. Was it possible for me to get into law school? I had barely passed my classes in high school and college, and had multiple arrests on my record. *Do they let criminals into law school?* Still, I thought law school would be the answer to all my problems. I'd finally get the approval of Triple B, be happy, have money, and achieve society's version of success.

Before I got ahead of myself though, the first step I had to take was to quit smoking weed—so I quit that cold turkey along with cigarettes. There was no way I could be a stoner and a law student.

Next I needed to take the LSAT, the law school entrance exam. The LSAT contained five parts, one of which was given twice: logical reasoning, analytical reasoning, reading comprehension, and an essay question. A perfect score on the LSAT was 180, and when I was applying to law school, a score of 155 would grant me acceptance to some schools. I went back to my ACT days and took the test without studying. I didn't even get close to 150. I took the test again, studying a bit on my own beforehand, and again didn't do well. Finally, I knew I had to do something different; after all, getting accepted into law school is a different game. I enrolled in an LSAT prep class and took the test a third time.

This time, I did well enough to get accepted to Thomas M. Cooley Law School at Western Michigan, located in Lansing, Michigan. Cooley gets a bad rap because it's not a top-tier law school. But my options were limited. It was an accredited law school willing to give me a chance, and I was grateful for the opportunity.

As part of the application process, I had to inform the school of all my criminal conduct, from juvenile to adult. I was to notify the school of all these incidents because, after graduation, when I applied to the bar, I'd have to pass a "character and fitness" evaluation to see if I was fit to be a lawyer. At that point, I would be asked to provide the state bar with the same information. With my questionable past and dismal college GPA, I thought my application would simply be thrown in the garbage, but, by some stroke of luck, I was accepted. However, the fact that the character and fitness evaluation was part of the bar exam haunted me every day of law school. I was afraid that I was wasting my time because even if I made it through, I wouldn't be able to pass the character and fitness exam to become a licensed attorney. The fear ate me up inside on a daily basis.

After only two short years in San Francisco, I moved back to the Midwest in the summer of 2006. My new destination was Lansing, Michigan, only a three-hour drive from my hometown of Cuyahoga Falls. This time, though, I flew cross-country. I still traveled light, leaving behind most of the belongings I had acquired in California.

Succeeding in law school was very different from succeeding in college, and I would need to do much more than just attend classes if I wanted to stay and pass. When I was an undergrad, I'd known how to play the game in order to get my degree. Law school was a different game entirely, and I didn't know the rules. I wasn't prepared. I hadn't been in school in over three years, and I didn't even know how to really study. Most of my classmates were younger, coming right out of college, and computer savvy. I hadn't done anything on a computer in quite some time other than play online poker and mess around on Myspace. Now I had to use a computer as a study aid.

Luckily I learned quickly, and I already knew how to type. I was serious about taking a different approach in law school. Because I didn't know how to succeed, I thought I would hang around the students who did know how to excel in school. To that end, I found the smartest students in our class, Brent and Dalton, and stuck to them like decal advertisements on a NASCAR stock racer.

Brent and Dalton were amazing study partners and amazing friends. They helped me stay focused, do the work, and put in long hours at the library. Most importantly, they didn't party a lot, so when I was with them, I was focused and clearheaded. They showed me how to create outlines for my classes, and we spent so much time teaching each other the law on a huge dry-erase board in empty classrooms on campus that we eventually had the subject memorized and knew it like the backs of our hands.

It wasn't just my memory skills that were enhanced, either. Law school taught me a different way of thinking, where not everything is black and white. It taught me to see situations and issues from both sides. Everything needed to be analyzed using the IRAC method:

- Issue—What is the issue here?

- Rule—What is the law that is applicable to the situation?
- Analysis—How is the law applied to the issue at hand?
- Conclusion—Why should a certain situation or set of facts be ruled on in a certain way?

My first semester in law school went okay, with me earning a B– average. And I thought, *That's not too bad for a kid who shouldn't even be in law school. At least I'm not failing out.* I was pleased with my score, so I decided to take on a heavier course load the following semester with the idea of getting out of law school earlier.

The problem was, when I wasn't with Brent and Dalton, I was hanging around people who drank a lot. We had season tickets to Michigan State football and tailgated every game. My grades suffered. In fact, I failed a class during my second semester and barely passed the others. When I got my grades back, I sat at my desk in my room, almost in tears. *What am I going to do?* I had put a lot of pressure on myself to succeed. Also, what would everyone else think? *No big surprise there. Kyle failed out of law school.* I felt like I'd let myself down and that Triple B was right: I was a loser and a failure.

To add to my stress, shortly after starting, I had started dating a girl who lived near my hometown. I made the three-hour drive to see her outside of Cuyahoga Falls almost every weekend. While I was there, I also spent some time with my high school buddies. Things got serious enough with this girl that I was sure we were in love. Unfortunately, I didn't know how to have a real relationship, and this one was filled with drama and constant fighting.

Eventually, we broke up, but we were still talking somewhat. Then one day, I got a call from one of my best high school friends, Chris.

"What's up?" I said, excited to chat.

"Listen, there's something I need to tell you," he said.

I knew this was serious because Chris never talked like this with me. I stood up from my kitchen table, leaving my bowl of oatmeal, and walked into my room. "What's going on?"

He proceeded to tell me that he was sleeping with my ex-girlfriend, who he knew I still cared for. He was the one I had confided in about my breakup with her and how much it was affecting me and I felt like he'd taken advantage of the situation.

The news hurt, even though I spent the next several months trying to get my ex back, just to stick it to Chris, which I eventually did. But it didn't make me feel any better. It was my ego that had taken a hit and that was what I was trying to salvage. I cared for her but we weren't really in love.

Although this situation was stressful, there was a silver lining in that I focused on school more to keep my inner thoughts from taking over, stuck with Brent and Dalton, and turned my grades around after that terrible second semester. By my last semester of law school, I made the dean's list and even earned a certificate of merit for getting the highest grade in a class.

I was so pleased with myself, and my mom was proud of me as well. I was sure that even Triple B would now recognize that I wasn't an idiot and that I was worthy of his love and acceptance. But that was not to be; I heard only crickets from him. I was slowly coming to the realization that I could discover the cure for cancer, and I would still never receive his acceptance or admiration.

Getting closer to graduation, I spent every day worrying about applying for and taking the bar exam because of what I would have to disclose about my past to the character and fitness board. In order to sleep at night I would tell myself that I wasn't going to practice law and I wouldn't even try to take the bar, instead I would attain a Juris Doctor and find some job.

To actually graduate from law school, I was required to take an externship at a law firm to learn real-life lawyering skills and be in a law firm environment. An externship is similar to an internship, I didn't get paid, it was a classroom experience outside of the school, and I was able to earn school credit for working. I knew I didn't want to stay in Michigan and I definitely didn't want to go back to Ohio. Therefore, I only applied to externships in New York City. I heard back from a boutique matrimonial law firm, and they accepted me. Of course they did; they really wanted the free labor.

My brother agreed to give me a ride, and just like that, I was off to New York City. I had visited it a few times before and was fascinated by it. It seemed like there were endless possibilities there for me to start a new life. It was like San Francisco all over again, and I was still searching for something more in myself.

CHAPTER 9
MOAB
I THINK WE'RE ALONE NOW

When I left Robin and Tahoe, I immediately drove back to Ohio without stopping anywhere else to explore. I was making the cross-country trip for the fourth time in as many months, and I was ready for some relaxation and time in my own bed again.

When I first got back to Ohio, Robin and I were communicating on a daily basis. Then it became every few days, and it dwindled from there. But then, one day, she messaged me to say she was heading out to Moab, Utah, in November to scout out some remote trails and asked me to join. Despite all the drama that had unfolded in Tahoe, I immediately agreed because I was still holding on to that hope that there was a chance for us. I understand this thinking was madness—but when I was in the moment I thought it was reasonable. Also, I was eager to go because this trip was going to be different to Washington and Tahoe. First of all, Paul wasn't going to be there. That was reason enough for me to go, to see what life was like without him around. Second, this was just a fun adventure so there wasn't the stress of a race and everything that comes with that—no aid stations to prep, no course to mark, no racers to deal with. We would just be exploring and checking out remote trails and seeing which were runnable. We would be tracking our mileage, camping out, and discovering what our legs were capable of running over a week or so in the desert—all for fun. There would only be a small group of us, and Debbie was going to rent an RV and follow us around to make our lives easier.

Before I left for Moab I was trying to make the most out of the time I had in Ohio. I focused on my business and signed up to run the Oil Creek 100 trail race in Titusville, Pennsylvania. I wanted to make sure I was in shape for Moab, and I wanted to challenge myself to run the one-hundred-mile distance, which I had never done before. I figured that I was somewhat ready for it, since I had been course-marking hundreds of miles out west at higher elevations. Despite my elevation training, Oil Creek wasn't going to be a breeze; it was a very tough course in its own right, with 17,785 feet of elevation change. The course consisted of a thirty-one-mile loop that runners circumnavigated three times and a shorter eight-mile loop, making it a little over one hundred miles.

Running one hundred miles is a lot more difficult than running fifty miles and takes a completely different mindset. During a fifty-mile race I could literally almost run the entire distance and not think too much about it. With a one-hundred-mile race, there needs to be more thought and preparation put into it. The rate of failure is much higher the longer the distance. I knew this because I had earned myself a DNF (Did Not Finish) during a previous one-hundred-mile attempt a few years back because I hadn't respected the distance. I went out too fast and got burned out in temperatures that reached almost ninety degrees. But this was a different race, a different year, and the weather would be much more cooperative. Also, I had the experience of my previous races and my time out west.

The day of the race the weather was mild and cool, although it was a bit humid in the morning. I took it slow, not caring about how fast I finished; I just wanted to finish it. I took the advice of one of my friends: "You should always feel like you're running too slow." I sure as hell felt like I was running slow. During the race, I had my usual low and high points but kept on pushing through the night, mentally focusing on just putting one step in front of the other. At one point in the middle of the race, I turned off my headlamp and couldn't see an inch in front of me—it was an eerie feeling. Sure, I wanted to give up countless times and wondered why I was putting myself through this pain, but I just kept telling myself, *This pain is temporary. Think of how you will feel at the finish. If you can run one hundred miles, you're capable of accomplishing anything. Come on, Come on, Come on!* I was basically fighting with myself, saying whatever I needed to just to convince my body to keep going and get to the finish line. Finally, I crossed the finish in the early hours the next morning, not terribly fast, though I did accomplish my goal and earn my first hundred-mile belt buckle. I sat down and a sense of relief washed over me. Suddenly, the pain was gone and all I could do was smile. However, an old knee injury from when I was a teenager had been aggravated during the race, and it was hurting a lot. I wasn't sure I'd be able to put a considerable number of miles on my knee while exploring Moab. Briefly, I considered whether to go or not—not only because of the knee, but for other obvious reasons—but only briefly.

Within a few days of finishing Oil Creek in early November, I headed toward Moab, Utah, in my trusty van. I had driven through Moab once a few years earlier with my cousin but we didn't stop to explore. I hadn't realized it was a mecca for outdoor enthusiasts. With endless trails, it's a paradise for mountain bikers, rock climbers, four-wheelers, and runners. This trip would be another opportunity for me to explore on foot a place the likes of which I had never seen before.

I told myself this adventure would be my last opportunity to see if I might have a future with Robin. No matter what happened there though, I was dead set on moving out west when all this was over. In that light, this Moab trip gave me another chance to see if I really liked the area.

I arrived in Moab before anyone else late in the evening. I pulled into the closest motel so I could use their Wi-Fi to do some work and catch some shut-eye. Brian arrived the next day, and we explored Moab together, just like we had Tahoe. Instead of running, to let my knee rest more, we drove around Arches National Park and Canyonlands National Park. The wilderness of the canyons, buttes, and arches was like a scene from a movie. Because it was the off-season it seemed like we had the entire parks to ourselves. Looking at the sun shine through the sixty-foot Delicate Arch reinforced my belief in a higher power. I thought some force or being must be behind such beauty.

Robin was supposed to arrive in a few days, and I wanted to get her something special so she knew I cared and thought about her. She occasionally smoked pot, so I thought it would be nice to get her some edible marijuana.

Because we couldn't just buy edibles from some random dude in Moab and we had time to kill, Brian and I gassed up the van, piled in, and went on a road trip to a weed shop.

Purchasing weed from a legal dispensary was quite the experience. Once we arrived, there was a "waiting room." It was similar to a doctor's waiting room, minus the chairs, magazines, and doctor. There were security cameras everywhere, and they checked our IDs and entered our information in their database. As I waited it felt like I was doing something nefarious on account of the screening processes we were subjected to. After everything checked out, we were directed into the next room through a glass door with a dark-green curtain.

When I swung open the door and moved the curtain aside, the stench of weed, which was a mix between a skunk's spray and burnt rope, hit me like a tidal wave. The "weed room" was set up like a jewelry store. Glass cases lined the perimeter of the room, but instead of diamonds and rubies, these cases were full of pot. I browsed around, reading the labels: Purple Haze, Green Lantern, Killer Kush, and so on. There were also refrigerators in the corners with glass doors that contained all kinds of edibles: everything from soda to candy bars made with marijuana. Behind the glass counters were the "budtenders." They were the experts on all the customers' marijuana needs. They looked like hippies, complete with dreadlocks and tie-dyed shirts. They were, in fact, very knowledgeable and able to answer any questions we had.

"I'm looking for an edible that's mellow and doesn't make me paranoid," I told the budtender as I walked up to one of the cases. It'd been years since I'd had an edible and I assumed I'd eat whatever I was getting Robin. Therefore, I wanted to get something that wouldn't freak me out.

She went over to the refrigerator and grabbed a few candy bars. "You'll like this cherry chocolate bar. It's got a nice, relaxing, chill buzz," she said, handing it to me.

Brian and I ended up getting a few cans of weed cola and a few chocolate bars. We didn't buy any smokable marijuana because we assumed Robin would already have some.

That afternoon, we drove straight back to Moab to meet Robin up in the Sand Flats Recreation Area, where we would be camping. Sand Flats was northeast of Moab and was elevated above the city. We got up to the campground and found that we had our pick of the lots on account of it being so late in the season. The campsites were different from those in Washington and Tahoe—instead of trees and grass the landscape was exposed and we were surrounded by dust and red rocks. I could see the La Sal Mountain peak to our east and miles of land surrounding us.

Soon, Brian and I had camp all set up, and we decided to have a few edibles to pass the time until Robin showed up. I ate a few bites of the chocolate bar on the advice of the budtender who'd said it wouldn't make me paranoid. After thirty minutes, I didn't feel anything, so I took another piece and so did Brian. By the time Robin arrived at the site an hour or so later, Brian and I were both wrecks: paranoid and high. She pulled into the site walked towards me and I greeted her with an awkward hug. The edibles had me so high, I wasn't sure how to act, and I hated that feeling of not being in control of my mind. She could tell something was up with us. I handed her the candy bar we'd gotten her and explained that we'd taken some edibles. She immediately understood why we were acting so weird.

It was getting late by the time she arrived, so she quickly set up her tent, and we all decided to go into town to have a drink and watch the 2016 presidential election results at the Moab Brewery.

Drinking a few beers and watching the results come in state by state, it became increasingly clear where the election was heading and it wasn't going as we, or anyone, expected. At least I'd been able to get my absentee ballot sent in months earlier. We finished up our beers and headed back to the site, and by this time the effects of the weed had all but vanished. We all went to sleep in our separate tents, and it felt like Robin and I were just old friends and nothing more—something I wanted to change.

We didn't think about the election much because it was easy to disconnect when we were out in the middle of the desert. In fact, we didn't think much about the election for a while after that night. Sure, we spoke about it in passing, but we weren't watching the news or keeping updated on the situation.

The next day, Brian, Robin, and I decided to go explore and run parts of the Whole Enchilada Trail, which starts at the La Sal Mountains and ends at the Colorado River. The trail was mostly used by mountain bikers, but we were going to run a dozen or so miles on it. Because the trail was an overall descent filled with loose rocks and boulders, it was a good opportunity to test out my knee and see if I would be able to run the rest of the week. After racing down the trail and reaching the Colorado River, my knee seemed to be holding up for the time being.

Moab's terrain made me feel like I was on a different planet. Although it was considered a desert, it wasn't filled with sand like I'd see in movies. It was more how I'd pictured what it might be like living on Mars. There were buttes and plateaus scattered across the dry red landscape. And then, almost coming out of nowhere, there were the La Sal Mountains, which had lush trees and vegetation.

Over the next few days, the old gang from Tahoe and Washington reunited: Brian, Robby, and Debbie. There were also a couple new faces, Matt and Nick, both of whom knew Robin from volunteering at previous races. Nick was tall with blond hair and blue eyes. He was there, as I would quickly realize, because he was interested in Robin as more than a friend, even though he was at least ten years her junior. I didn't want to fight for Robin's attention again, so Nick was an unexpected, unwanted surprise.

Once everyone was in Moab, we started planning where we were going to explore right away. Robin, Nick, Matt, and I headed north from Swanny City Park toward the trails that led to the Colorado River. The plan was to explore thirty or so miles and meet up with the rest of the group at the end of the trails. Brian and Robby stayed back because they weren't up for the long mileage yet and were just there to keep Debbie company. Debbie, who was driving the RV, would keep our bellies filled and meet us at the end of the runs just like the Auntie she is.

Exploring was very different from course-marking: we only had a rough idea of what we wanted to do and we weren't sure of the mileage, or where we were going. Also, we had to overpack food and water in case we were out there longer than anticipated. We were exposed to the sun a great deal. It wasn't brutally hot in November but could reach the eighties at times, and there wasn't much shade to protect us.

After thirty miles the first day, we met everyone back at camp where Debbie had arrived. Because the RV only

slept five or so, some of us would be sleeping in tents. Brian and Robby had already set up everyone's tents while we were running, so that night, we didn't have to make any decisions about who'd sleep where. Later that evening, we all sat around the campfire and had a few beers. I started passing out my extra edibles because I was trying to get rid of them. After my experience earlier, I knew I would never take another one again. I was anticipating everyone freaking out, like I had, but everyone just seemed to get sleepy. This wasn't a bad thing though, as we had to get some shut-eye, because the next day, Matt, Robin, Nick, and I would be exploring another thirty miles.

Robin and I had been together for about three days in Moab by now, and we hadn't had any physical contact other than that first hug. I decided to change that. The next evening, before everyone went to bed, I saw Robin outside by the fire. Nobody was around, so I took her arm, pulled her close to me, and we kissed.

Soon after the kiss, it was time to figure out where everyone would be sleeping that night. To my delight, Robin suggested that she and I sleep together in the back of the RV. Nick didn't take too kindly to Robin's suggestion. In fact, he put his sleeping bag and clothes on the back bed where Robin and I were going to be sleeping. I explained that I was going to be the one sleeping there, and eventually he moved his belongings. I spoke to Robin about it, but she just blew it off as Nick being young and naïve. That night, Robin and I slept next to each other, but we didn't do anything. Well, technically, Robin made a move by putting her hand on my leg, but I didn't respond because I thought it had been an accident.

I could understand why Nick wanted to be with Robin: she was beautiful, loved trail running, and had asked him to come hang out in Moab. But in addition to putting his belongings in the back of the RV, he often did weird shit, and gave off a creepy vibe. For example, right after the RV first showed up, we were all hanging out in it, and Nick put his head on Robin's lap out of the blue. She looked around at the rest of us as if she was weirded out. We were all weirded out. He then started referring to me as "Dad" and Robin as "Mom." Even after he figured out that Robin and I were together—whatever that meant—he wouldn't stop flirting with her.

The day after Robin and I spent the night together for the first time in the RV, we went out exploring again, and I was in a good mood because I had just learned that Nick and Matt would be leaving that night. I wouldn't have to worry about Nick hitting on Robin again. Really, this just spoke of my insecurity. I shouldn't have cared, but I wasn't confident that Robin wouldn't be agreeable to Nick's advances. I was now in the same situation Paul had been in with me. Even as all this was going on, I knew that being with Robin wasn't a good idea, but I didn't think I deserved better. Besides, I was in the middle of nowhere and needed to make the best of the situation. At least, that's what I told myself.

As the miles increased, my knee was really starting to act up again. Combined with running with Brian and Robin before the crew got there, I had put over one hundred miles on my legs in just a few days. I shouldn't have been running, but I didn't want to stay behind at camp. I ended up going out running again for thirty more miles, using trekking poles as assistance. It was the last of my exploring trails in Moab as my knee finally surrendered and ballooned to the size of a cantaloupe.

That evening, we had a fire as usual and some beers. We also, thankfully, said goodbye to Nick and Matt. After they left, it was like a weight had been lifted off my shoulders. I didn't have to worry about him or his advances anymore. But I didn't entirely trust Robin, either after everything I had witnessed and experienced with her.

After they left, we retired to the RV. Robin and I were sharing the back bed again. She made the same move she had made the night before by touching my leg. This time, I reciprocated and touched her back and we ended up going all the way again in the rear of the RV, which was interesting because there were three or four other people sleeping in the front, separated by only a curtain.

The next morning was different, not because I had slept with Robin again, but because it was the first time I wouldn't be going out running on the trails, due to my knee. Brian had an electroshock therapy device that was supposed to help my knee recover, but it didn't seem to do much. I think it was too injured to improve that quickly. I had never stayed behind before. It was good though, because this gave Robby and Brian an opportunity to explore Moab while I stayed with Debbie to keep her company, and we were able to catch up and talk about her races. It was nice because Debbie knew my entire history with Robin and it felt good to talk about my concerns. We also talked about how weird Nick was, how everyone else sensed the same and how she hoped he wouldn't be at her races.

That day, Robin's crew got lost while exploring and ended up "borrowing" an abandoned RV and riding in it until they found civilization. Debbie and I knew something had happened to them when they didn't meet us at the designated spot even hours past the time they were supposed to arrive. We were getting a little bit concerned and contemplated calling the authorities, but we knew Robin was an experienced outdoorswoman, so we held off. Eventually, they arrived and were so excited about what they had gone through that they couldn't stop talking. For a moment I was jealous that I had missed out on that run, but was glad others were having an exciting adventure of their own. When Robin saw me, she actually gave me a hug, which was weird, because she usually didn't hug anyone in public ever. It was as if we were officially together and she was letting everyone else know. Or so I chose to believe. But really, I was just trying to convince myself that Robin truly cared for me; I was holding on to whatever scrap I could.

That night, we all drove back to the Sand Flats where we had initially stayed on election night. We made a big pasta meal because it was the last night with the RV and almost everyone would be leaving in the morning. Only Brian, Robby, Robin, and I would stay. We made a fire, ate, and drank beer.

No one would be staying in the RV that evening because Debbie was leaving late that night to take it back so I went to set up my tent. I was sort of assuming that Robin would be staying with me; we had slept together the past two nights in the RV, and things seemed to be going well. But then Robin started to set up her own tent. I was dumbfounded and confronted her about it. "Why are you setting up your tent?"

"What do you mean? Where am I going to stay?"

"With me, of course. Why wouldn't you?" I asked.

"That's all you needed to say."

Robin told me later that she wanted me to take control of the situation and just tell her where she was staying. She said she liked it when I was confident. In reality, I don't think she felt like pitching her own tent. We ended up sleeping in my tent—but it was a wild and windy night, so we didn't get much sleep.

In the morning, before the day's activities, we grabbed breakfast at Eklecticafe, an intimate little local coffee shop with an outdoor patio on the edge of Moab. Robin wanted to mountain-bike the Whole Enchilada, so Brian, Robby, and I decided to climb a mountain in the La Sal range. My knee was feeling better by then, and I knew I could handle it.

We dropped Robin off at the top of the Whole Enchilada Trail then headed toward the mountain. We didn't have a plan yet; we were just driving. When we saw a high peak, we simply parked and decided to try and summit it. None of us had proper climbing gear, such as coats and water bottles, but we decided to go ahead anyway. The terrain was difficult and littered with loose rocks and it was getting colder as we climbed higher. Brian and I kept pushing, but it was getting dangerous and Robby held back. We made it up to around 12,500 feet before we decided to stop and head back down.

That night we met back up with Robin and went out for some beers and food at a burger place in Moab. Robin decided that she didn't want to camp out again, so she found a nice Airbnb with a hot tub. When the four of us arrived, we all headed straight for the hot tub without discussing sleeping arrangements. There were two beds upstairs, which were divided by a partition, plus a couch downstairs. Brian soon went to sleep on one of the beds upstairs, and Robby took the couch. I told Robin that I would be sleeping with her in the other bed upstairs. She immediately agreed.

Robin and I were intimate that night and again in the morning. The morning was good because it was one of the first times we'd slept together when alcohol wasn't involved. I thought that was progress for our relationship.

Robin could sometimes flip like a switch. She could be very nice to me one minute, and then act like I or anyone else didn't exist the next. That day, she hit the switch and pretended I was nothing to her. I'd ask her questions and she would respond with one-word answers or not at all. It seemed like she wanted to be as far away from me and everyone else as possible. After breakfast, Robin sat at the dining room table, working on her computer and ignoring everyone else, including me. This was just the way she was sometimes.

We had to be out of the house by that afternoon. Brian and Robby were going back home. I, obviously, would stick around if Robin wanted me to. There were still a few trails in Moab she wanted to explore. Even though I wasn't able to go on the trails with her because my knee was injured from climbing the mountain, she asked me to stay in Moab with her for a few more days. I don't think she wanted to go back home to Paul quite yet.

So after Brian and Robby left, it was just me and Robin. This was the first time we had been alone together since our last day in Washington months ago. It was an odd feeling. There was nobody to hide behind and nobody else to talk to.

On our first day alone, Robin went for a run and while she was gone, I needed to find a new place for us to stay because our current Airbnb was already booked up, and it was too big for us anyway. We didn't want to camp anymore, so I found a nice modern condo with all the amenities, the most important of which was the washer and dryer. It was relatively cheap, due to it being the off-season, and it was also within walking distance of downtown and the bars, which we would also take full advantage of.

Robin met me at the condo later that day after her run, and she seemed quite pleased with the place I'd rented. We decided to go out for dinner that night and settled on Blu Pig, a barbecue and blues joint. When we arrived, I slid down on one side of a booth and Robin sat down right next to me. I'd never seen her show this much affection before. Her switch had been flipped again. *Maybe this is how she is when nobody's around and she actually likes someone*, I thought hopefully. We were definitely acting like a couple.

As we talked, things became so serious that we decided to make our relationship "Facebook official," which might seem odd, since she was married. However, she wasn't even Facebook friends with Paul, let alone officially listed as married to him, so she thought it might be okay. We both changed our Facebook status to "In a Relationship" with each other - now the entire world knew about us. It was official now: we were in love! Well, kind of, but I was definitely infatuated. And we did tell each other that we loved one another. I definitely loved the adventure and the high she had me on. I didn't understand the ramifications of posting our status on Facebook and what other people would think, nor how it would impact Paul if he found out.

After dinner, we headed back to the condo, fooled around, and went to bed.

Robin deleted the post announcing our new relationship on her Facebook page early the next morning, but she kept our relationship status as it was. She said she didn't want to call attention to it. That did hurt a little, but we were still Facebook official.

We spent the whole week in Moab, going out to eat, drinking, and sleeping together. When our rental period was up, neither of us wanted to head back to our regular lives yet, so we decided to camp out for one last night up at the Sand Flats again. We didn't go out that night; we just stayed at our campsite, had a few drinks, and hung around the campfire. Everything seemed to be going well.

Then she got an email from Paul with a message to the effect of "What the fuck?". He'd also included a screenshot of our relationship status from Facebook—a picture of me and a picture of Robin with a caption that read, "Robin Is in a Relationship with Kyle." Someone had obviously seen the status on Robin's page and sent it to Paul. The odd thing was that he hadn't received it until two or three days after it had been posted.

Robin was freaking out, to say the least. She didn't know what to do. She tried to call him, but he didn't pick up so she considered leaving that night. She was concerned about what he might do to her things in the house, or that he might sabotage her life somehow. Eventually, after a few beers, she calmed down a little and we fell asleep.

The next morning, we went to Eklecticafe again for breakfast so she could assess the situation with Paul. He had left several voicemails during the night, threatening to make her life difficult. I advised her not to go back to Tahoe and to let him cool off for a bit. She was talking about getting a divorce attorney and wasn't sure what to do.

In addition to all this, she was planning on spending Thanksgiving with her son and the holiday was fast approaching. Her son lived near Portland, Oregon with his father. She ultimately decided not to go back to Tahoe just yet, but instead to rent a house in Eugene, Oregon for a week and swing by and pick up her son on the way there. Robin had spent a lot of time in Eugene, used to live there, and had friends in the area. She invited me to go with her, and I accepted.

CHAPTER 10
NYC
I GET BY WITH A LITTLE HELP FROM MY FRIENDS

Sully had just landed the plane in the Hudson, President Obama was about to be inaugurated as the first African-American president, and I was learning the harsh reality of law-firm life.

Right before I moved to New York City, I had found a place on Craigslist. It was in Soho at 42 Howard Street, just a block from Chinatown in Manhattan. The ad claimed it was a furnished one-bedroom for $900 a month, which sounded like an amazing deal for NYC. I should have known then something was fishy. I sent the money, sight unseen. Again I moved with only a suitcase of clothes. When I arrived, I quickly discovered why the rent was so affordable.

I walked up the three flights of stairs to the unit and knocked on the door. After almost ten minutes of knocking, a short, pudgy, Asian guy with dark hair answered. It was clear that I had woken him. He let me in and showed me around. The place was essentially an open area with two bedrooms, one on each side, and with a small kitchen right inside the door off the bathroom. I thought this was odd, because there were only two bedrooms, and I knew there would be three people living there, including myself. Then I was directed toward my living space. It was a loft bed in the living room separated by a partition. In addition, the day I arrived, there was a French foreign-exchange student sleeping in my bed! I eventually got my bed but was still underwhelmed. However, I was there, and there was no turning back.

I wouldn't be getting paid at the law firm because I was receiving course credit, and student loans could only pay for so much—this was New York City, after all—so I needed to find a job. As I had in San Francisco, I applied to be a server at several restaurants. I was rather taken aback when some places actually asked for a headshot when applying. Within a few days though, I got a job as a server at Applebee's. It was located downtown in Battery Park, just a stone's throw away from the Word Trade Center. At the time, construction on the new building and memorial was still under way. Every day, the construction workers filed into Applebee's around noon with their hard hats and ordered lunch. Sometimes, they'd sneak in a beer or two.

My legal externship at the matrimonial law firm was on Fifth Avenue in midtown Manhattan. It had two partners and one associate. I worked at the law firm during the week and at Applebee's on the weekend. During that period, I worked over a hundred days straight without a day off. At first I was hoping the firm would offer me a job after the externship. I quickly realized that they never had any intention of doing so.

My experience at the law firm was, to put it bluntly, awful. My work station was the size of a small closet, and situated just outside one of the partner's office. I am still haunted by the sound of Leon's voice calling me into his office on a daily basis just so he could hear himself talk.

Leon was an older, heavyset, bald gentleman who wore sweaters every day, and looked like an injured penguin waddling around when he walked. He should have been retired already; he had made a fortune in the hotel business and wasn't doing much legal work in the firm at all.

I would hear Leon's shrieking voice before I even set my bag down in the morning: "Kyle! You here yet? Get in here! Why are you so late?" He would shout this at me even though I got in before eight a.m. every day and didn't have to be there until nine.

I quickly learned that I always needed to bring a notepad and pen into Leon's office so I could pretend to write down whatever nonsense he was spewing. It was never actually important and didn't have anything to do with the law, but he liked to see me take notes on what he said. Sometimes it was about a movie he had seen or a restaurant he had eaten at. I didn't learn anything about the law from him.

When I wasn't in Leon's office, the other partner, Barry, would give me contracts to proofread or send me on errands at the courthouse. The firm basically used me for my free access to Westlaw—a computer-based legal research website. Westlaw can be very expensive, but as a law student, I had access to it for free.

The lawyers were also billing their clients for the work I did. According to their invoices, I was worth $250 an hour. The attorneys were chasing down their clients to get paid more than they were actually trying cases. Billable hours was the name of the game.

The partners made a lot of money, but they were miserable. Spending sixty to seventy hours a week at something they hated didn't seem like a life. *If this is success, I don't want any part of it*, I thought. It was also depressing to work with the clients. Husbands and wives getting a divorce would often fight over petty things like silverware and pets more than they would fight over custody of their own children. It got to the point where I was actually looking forward to my weekends at Applebee's.

The pressure of working every day, not being sure if I was going to be able to take the bar exam, and sleeping in the middle of a living room was beginning to take a toll on me. I started experiencing severe panic attacks on a daily basis. Once, after a long day at the law firm, I got on the subway to head home. The car was crowded and I made my way toward the door between the train cars and leaned up against it. Suddenly, a rush came over me. My heart started beating very fast, my palms started sweating, I couldn't think straight, and I was having trouble breathing. I squatted down and put my head between my knees. I didn't understand what was going on, and all I could do was pray that it would just end. I stayed in that position until my stop. I slowly got up, pushed my way through the crowd to the open doors, and squeezed out. The attack started to subside once I climbed out of the subway tunnel and hit the fresh air. But I was scared and worried about what I had just experienced.

After that, panic attacks became a daily occurrence for me. Usually, they would start around the same time: while I was at the law firm in the afternoon. I didn't seek help, because I had neither the time nor the health insurance to cover the costs of medical attention. I popped ibuprofen like Tic Tacs to keep the attacks under control. I continued to wonder what was wrong but kept telling myself that the externship would soon end and hopefully so would the panic attacks. I just wanted to get away and not have to go back to the law firm. *Is this what living in New York City is all about? Do I not have what it takes to live here?*

At long last, my externship was over, and I could graduate from law school. I headed back to Michigan to get my degree. The day of my graduation ceremony, as I sat waiting to receive my degree, I felt my palms start to sweat. I knew what was about to happen: I was going to have a severe panic attack. Looking around, everyone else seemed so happy and excited, while I just wanted this attack to subside. I was able to get myself together in time to walk across the stage and receive my degree, but I wasn't able to enjoy or remember the moment because I was so focused on not losing my shit. It was probably due to the fear and uncertainty of what I was going to do with my life. Yes, I had graduated from law school, but I still wasn't sure if I would be able to take the bar and pass the character and fitness evaluation. Triple B attended the ceremony and told me afterward: "Quite the accomplishment, I would have lost a bet."

After graduation, my panic attacks seemed to subside and I decided to return to New York City, risk everything, and take the bar exam. After all, what did I have to lose? I would focus on passing the bar exam first and go from there. To study for the exam, most aspiring lawyers sign up for a course, which costs around $3,000. I thought that was silly. After three years of law school, I had to pay thousands of dollars more just to study for an exam I had thought I was studying for over the past three years? I decided to forgo the bar course, partly because I didn't have the cash and partly because I thought it didn't really matter if I passed the bar, because I was sure I wouldn't be able to pass the character and fitness evaluation. I studied half-heartedly and took the exam.

The exam was held at the Jacob Javits Convention Center, a huge glass building on the banks of the Hudson River. Thousands of wannabe attorneys filed into this huge space that was normally used for expos and conventions. That particular day, the floor was filled with hundreds of tables and chairs. Once everyone took their seats, massive garage doors closed down all around us. When the exam was over, I quickly exited the building to get some air. I knew I had failed, and that was confirmed a few weeks later.

By this time, I was working in New Jersey at LexisNexis, a legal research and publishing company, as a customer support representative and I had moved out of my "room" in Soho and was living in a proper apartment in Hell's Kitchen. The job didn't pay much, and I had to borrow money sometimes from my mother to make ends meet. It was over an hour-long commute from the Port Authority out to New Jersey for work, and I would get up three hours early every day and take the train in. This strategy was a success, as I was never once late.

I decided to try the bar exam again and actually take the prep course this time. I also quit working at Applebee's so I could focus on studying more. After I took the train home each day, I would walk from the Port Authority to the New York Public Library and study until they closed. On the weekends, I would go to the bar prep class and then study at Starbucks or the library. Neither place was particularly conducive to studying. Starbucks had too much noise and activity, and the New York Public Library wasn't all that quiet, either. More often than not, there were more people in there sleeping and getting kicked out than actually studying. Still, I wasn't going to let myself take the bar exam again without giving it my all, which I hadn't done the first time.

The weekends and long nights paid off. I passed the New York bar exam on my second attempt. Of course, this would still mean nothing if I wasn't able to get through the character and fitness evaluation.

With regard to my character and fitness, I had a long history of immoral conduct. But I wasn't that person anymore. I thought that if I had got this far, why couldn't I go a bit farther? I decided to disclose everything I had ever done wrong to the New York bar, as is required.

In applying to be admitted to the bar, not only did I need to disclose my criminal conduct, but I also had to disclose my juvenile criminal conduct and even minor speeding tickets. It was going to take me some time to amass all of this information. I had to fly back to Ohio and visit each individual police station I had been arrested at and get certified copies of the police report, my arrest record, and the results of each case. I had to do this for each instance of disorderly conduct, underage drinking, disturbing the peace, speeding tickets, assault, driving under a suspended license, hit and skip, and driving under the influence. I submitted it all to the New York State Bar and crossed my fingers.

After all the information is submitted, every applicant has to be interviewed by an upstanding member of the bar or officer of the court, like a judge or prosecutor, to ensure that they really are fit for to be an attorney.

The day of my interview came, and I showed up just like everyone else. There were hundreds of us being interviewed that day. We all sat in a huge room on the twenty-sixth floor in the building for the Committee on Character and Fitness on Madison Avenue, and they would call about ten of us at a time into another room, where we would wait to be interviewed. From within the second room, I could see the applicants getting interviewed through a window on the other side. It seemed that each interview was taking about five minutes or so.

When I was called into the second room, I sat there for quite some time. At least an hour passed, and I grew increasingly nervous as everyone else was called into their respective interviews. I found out later that they were waiting for a "special" prosecutor to interview me.

Finally, they called my name. As a clerk grabbed my file from a shelf I noticed it was covered with all sorts of red markings and notes. I was led over to a woman who introduced herself as a prosecutor and the clerk handed her the thick folder. I sat down in front of her and she started going through my records and pulling out papers, barely looking up at me. She sat there, not saying a word, for an eternity. It felt like a lifetime was passing by as she read the papers and pushed them to the side.

Then she pulled out one paper and focused on it, examining it in great detail. She finally asked me, "I see you recently got caught speeding?"

"Yes," I answered, surprised. "I was late for class in law school and didn't want to miss anything."

She looked into my eyes and said, "How do I know you're not going to make this same mistake again?"

Without thinking, I replied, "Now that I live in New York City, I don't have a car anymore, so I won't be driving."

She continued to thumb through my paperwork. Without looking up at me, she said, "You have quite the file here. Are you going to be an upstanding and honest attorney?"

"Yes, if given the chance."

"Okay then," she said, signing a paper. "You're all set. Congratulations."

It was as if a weight had been lifted off my shoulders. I couldn't think or breathe, but it wasn't because of a panic attack this time. I was in! I had passed the character and fitness evaluation. The next day, I was sworn in as a lawyer and officer of the court at the historic First Judicial Department of the Appellate Division of the Supreme Court building: I, Kyle Victor Robinson, who had taken six years to graduate high school, gone to drug rehab, been arrested countless times, almost failed out of college, and been written off as a loser, was a licensed New York attorney!

Now that I was a licensed attorney, I thought I'd try my hand at actually practicing law. I probably applied for over one hundred jobs and received either polite rejections or silence. I did get an interview or two but never heard back. At first, I kept all my rejection letters, as if I was going to use them as motivation to get a law job.

I wasn't even really sure if I wanted to practice law after my experience at my externship. On the other hand, that might have been something I told myself to make it okay that I hadn't found a job practicing law. Because, at the time, I did want a job practicing law. It's what I had gone to school for. The problem was, I didn't have the experience or the grades, and the legal market was currently in the toilet.

Even though I couldn't find a job practicing law, I did want to at least find a job in the city that paid more than I was currently making. I applied to jobs where a law degree was "preferred." Eventually, I found employment in downtown Manhattan as an account executive selling legal services and electronic discovery equipment for lawyers. No more train rides out to New Jersey. Basically, law firms would give us boxes and boxes of legal papers, which we would condense down to a single disc. I went from client to client, picking up and dropping off boxes. Back at the office, I made cold calls to law firms asking them if they needed our services. I didn't like the job at all, and it didn't fulfill me, but at least I was a little more content. I was working in the city and was able to make a living.

I continued looking for a job that I would actually enjoy though. I wanted something that would challenge me and allow me to grow as a person. To that end, I landed an interview with an online continuing education company. Professionals have to take courses to maintain their license, and this company provided such courses through their website. It seemed like a good fit for me. The company had an award-winning culture, and they seemed to be excited about me as a potential employee. When I received the offer, it was a pay cut from what I was currently making, but I didn't care because I was more concerned about working in a great environment and actually using my degree. I was brought on as a program attorney and would help develop and facilitate legal education courses.

Although the company wasn't a start-up, it had a start-up atmosphere and there were fewer than twenty employees. Everyone was young, including the president and CEO (he was the same age as me), and we were all crammed into small offices in a building in the financial district in downtown NYC, working together to create online content. My desk was in an office in the back, which I shared with three other employees.

This job was like no other I'd had. It gave me the freedom to work how I wanted without a boss micromanaging me. I worked in an atmosphere where someone believed in me, encouraged me to do good things, and actually wanted to see me succeed. In fact, the president of the company, Gary, would go on to become one of my best friends, my mentor, and somebody who showed me that I was capable of much more than I thought I was.

I no longer dreaded getting up in the morning to go to work. I looked forward to seeing everyone at the office. I believe it's because I was actually creating something. Nobody was breathing down my neck, telling me what to do and how to do it, and I didn't have the stress of a sales quota to meet. Although my primary job was to create legal content for the company, I was permitted to do so much more.

The best part of the job was the opportunity to do non-job-related things. Employees were allowed and even encouraged to address the company at the morning meeting on whatever they liked and I took full advantage. My presentations tended to focus on health, wellness, and personal development. Once, I gave a presentation titled "Kyle's Kool-Aid: Twelve Secrets to Happiness." My twelve secrets were:

1. Everyone deserves a second chance;
2. Say sorry even when it's not your fault;
3. Be thankful;
4. Keep an open mind;
5. Chase your fear;
6. The past does not predict the future;
7. Take 100% responsibility for your life;
8. Laugh;

9. Keep positive people around you;
10. Believe in and be yourself;
11. Make your bed every morning; and
12. Above all, love yourself and be kind to others.

It was the first opportunity I'd ever had to share my story and where I had come from. Although I didn't go into much detail, I did vaguely reference some of my struggles.

In addition to this, I presented a workshop on goals, which involved everyone writing down their goals and how they would achieve them, and I also had an opportunity to lead a workshop on optimism and seeing the brighter side of things. My life was turning into something I had never even imagined it could be; I was actually developing and creating my life, instead of letting it create me. In time, I was given a supervisory role, which I'd never had before. I directly supervised the interns we hired and was involved in the employee hiring and interview process.

I thought I had finally made it and I would never leave this place. I worked long hours and came in on the weekends. Having someone actually believe in me and in my abilities was a life-changing confidence boost. It was as if everything I had dreamed of was coming to fruition.

For the first time in my life, I had friends who wanted the best for me and were rooting for me. I had never known what that was like before. There were two individuals in particular who shaped me during that time: Gary and Joseph. If it wasn't for their guidance, friendship, and mentoring, I wouldn't have eventually found my true voice or my authentic self.

Joseph was the company's video producer, and he was responsible for all the filming, editing, and audio aspects of our material. I worked very closely with him to develop our legal programs and got to know him very well. Joseph has a number of unique abilities that make him an extraordinary human being, many of which anyone would be able to see within five minutes of meeting him.

First, he's a very hard worker. I don't mean in the sense that he will work all day and all night to get a job done. He'll do that, too, but he will also make sure the job is done exactly right. Time and time again, I have witnessed him go back over a particular program or video setup just to get it perfect. If it takes extra hours or even if the project needs to be done over again from scratch, that's what he'll do. Many people won't do that; Joseph will not only do it, he'll do it without complaint.

Second, Joseph is passionate about feminism and women's rights, more so than anyone else I know. His beliefs have only given me a deeper awareness of the atrocities and horrors related to sexism all around me. I now see the world in a different way because of him. Every time he talked about feminism, I could see the passion in his eyes and hear it in his voice. He is truly making a difference and I am living proof.

Finally, and this attribute is the one I believe makes Joseph so special and is the reason he is one of the most amazing people I know: simply put, he doesn't judge people or situations. That is, from my perspective, he treats everyone with respect no matter who they are or how they look. He gives them the benefit of the doubt every time. This quality is the one I most want to possess, and he has it. When my sister and I catch each other judging people or situations, we always say, "What would Joseph do?" to each other. I really do try to think about what Joseph would do or think in certain situations, and I then know how to act. This nonjudgmental approach is what makes Joseph, Joseph.

Gary, the president of the company, has a confidence I crave. Like me, Gary is a licensed attorney in New York but decided not to practice. He wanted something more out of life and had the passion and drive to go after it. He is the one who sparked something in me that pushed me to achieve greater things. Like Joseph, Gary possesses qualities that I truly admire.

First of all, he is eager to learn. Gary always says, "Teaching is the best form of learning." Basically, if you want to learn something very well, explain it to someone else. That's one of the reasons why I presented a program on happiness, optimism, and goals to the company—because I wanted to learn more about them myself. Gary is an avid reader, and he inspired me to get my hands on as many books as possible. He recommended books that had a huge impact on the way I live my life and how I think, such as *The Alchemist* by Paulo Coelho, *The Autobiography of a Yogi* by Paramahansa Yogananda, and *Tuesdays with Morrie* by Mitch Albom. Gary's attitude toward learning came from a desire to become a better person, which is something I crave as well. I believe that's one reason why we get along so well.

Second, Gary isn't afraid to speak his mind. This can be both negative and positive. I always knew where I stood with Gary. If he didn't like something someone did or if he didn't think much of it, he would let them know. After I did my presentation on optimism for the company, I was feeling down because I felt it hadn't gone well and I could have done better. I went into Gary's office and asked him what he thought. I was searching for something positive, but he informed me that it was one of the worst presentations he had ever seen. He didn't think much of my public speaking skills, and he let me know it. I left his office feeling like a piece of garbage but it inspired me to try harder. However, at the same time, he could buoy me up, encourage me, and make me feel good about my work, who I was, and where I was heading in life. He is the one who always encouraged me to think outside the box, so to speak.

Finally, Gary isn't afraid to take risks. He will try anything to see what results are possible. We started a business venture together while I was working with him—a start-up school for start-up businesses—and it was a complete disaster. But he didn't see it as a failure, instead he used the lessons he learned to make himself a better leader. He will take risks no matter what other people think. He simply doesn't care. I want that ability.

I really got to know Gary well when we trained to run a marathon together. I had started running on a regular basis in law school, which my sister had initially sparked. Gary renewed my passion for running. He had never run a marathon before, and I was ready for another one, so we signed up for the Philadelphia Marathon and trained together. Training for that sort of race meant we spent a lot of time together. We both lived in Brooklyn at the time, I in Crown Heights, and he in Park Slope. I would run over to his house on the weekends, and we would go for our long runs through the city streets. It was like a video game avoiding cabs, people, and open doors. Since we worked together, we would run home from work, too.

Even though running took up a lot of my time, it seemed like I was more focused on work and was being more productive than ever. Still, in time, I decided that I needed to move on from Gary's company and this job that I loved so much.

There was still something inside of me yearning for more, and this job wasn't providing me with it. I wasn't sure what I was looking for, but I wanted more freedom. I wanted to be able to get up in the morning and do exactly what I wanted to do. And I had learned that if that was what I truly wanted, all I needed to do was create it.

Plus, something just rubbed me wrong about working my butt off for someone else's company. If I wanted to work that hard, it should have been for myself and for something I was passionate about. There were new employees at the company by then who had more "fire" than I did at the time. They were a better fit for my role, and I was ready to step aside and let them lead.

My time in New York was coming to an end. I had been there almost five years, and I wasn't the same insecure person I had been when I arrived. I'd look out the window from the nineteenth floor down on Broadway in downtown Manhattan and see waves of people walking. To me, they looked carefree, and more importantly, they weren't chained to a desk. I wondered why they didn't have jobs, or if they did, what they did that gave them such freedom to be out in the middle of the day. I understood they all had their own stories and problems to deal with, but I fantasized that they were all free and doing whatever they wanted outside of an office, and I wanted the same.

Gary and I mutually agreed it was time for me to move on from the company—so he let me go to enable me to receive unemployment benefits. Leaving was bittersweet. At the time, I thought that perhaps New York had gotten the better of me, because I hadn't been there that long, but the honest truth was that I needed different challenges in my life in order to grow. I had had many valuable experiences in New York that had become part of who I was and shaped me as a person—a better person. Life just had something different in store for me, and I needed to find out what that was. I decided to move back to Ohio without a job or any job prospects.

CHAPTER 11
EUGENE
FAMILY MAN

The day before Robin and I left Moab, we drove up toward the La Sal Mountains. A thick layer of snow, which blanketed the mountains and the trees below them, greeted us. Winter was fast approaching, and Thanksgiving was only a week away. The next day, Robin and I packed up our vehicles and headed north from Moab to Eugene, separately, to celebrate the holiday with her son and her friends.

Eugene, Oregon, is about sixty miles east of the Pacific Ocean, and the drive took about sixteens hours, which was long enough that I needed to stop and sleep on the way. I didn't mind the drive so much because I wasn't on I-80 or I-90 the entire way, and I got to see some new parts of the Pacific Northwest for the first time. I arrived in Eugene before Robin because she needed to pick up her son on the way. This gave me some time to check out the town.

While we drove, we stayed in constant contact, trying to figure out where we would be staying when we got there. We needed to find a vacation rental on short notice during Thanksgiving week that was big enough for the three of us. Plus, Robin was planning on inviting her friends and their kids over for a Friendsgiving, and she wanted to make an impression, so finding a nice place was also paramount. Eventually, she settled on a Fern Ridge Lake beach house located west of Eugene with a private beach. This was ideal for everyone. Robin's kid would be able to take advantage of the beach, there were hiking and running trails nearby, and the place would even impress Robin's friends.

Once in Eugene, I needed to kill time so I decided to check out our vacation rental before exploring the city. Pulling into the driveway, I noticed a car parked out front and later discovered the woman who was renting it out to us was still there, preparing the place and dropping off some groceries and amenities.

The house was impressive, with a wrap-around rear balcony with a view of the Fern Ridge Lake. On the first floor was a fireplace, a den, a living room, two bedrooms—one for Robin's kid, and a kitchen. In the center of the home was a spiral staircase that led down to two more bedrooms and a laundry room. Robin and I would share one room downstairs, and the other would remain empty our entire stay. On the kitchen counter were a variety of cheeses, coffee, wine, and other goodies that the owner was leaving for us.

As I was exploring the house, a woman emerged from the dining room, and I immediately introduced myself. "I'm Kyle. I'm renting this place with Robin," I said, holding out my hand.

"Oh, you're her husband, then? This will be a great family vacation for you!" she responded, excited.

That was a phrase I wasn't ready for, or used to hearing, and I wasn't sure how to react. "Yes, we're looking forward to this week," I replied, not wanting to explain the complicated situation. Then I started thinking that if for some reason I had to explain it, it would all sound incredibly fucked up: *No, I just met Robin a little over five months ago. I'm just the guy she's cheating on her husband with. We decided it was time for us to spend Thanksgiving together and for me to meet her son and all her friends for the first time. That's not out of the ordinary, right?*

I dropped off my bags and left to check out Eugene and pick up some supplies, and by "supplies" I mean beer. Robin and other runners had described the area around Eugene as some sort of outdoor trail-running paradise. Like many cities, it had the usual grocery stores and bars, and a quaint downtown. What made it unique though is that it was located close to the Pacific Ocean. The area was filled with lush trees, mountains, and miles of running trails. I quickly fell in love with the place.

As I drove around, I realized that I hadn't seen the sun in quite some time. There had been almost constant cloud cover and a lot of rain since I got to the Pacific Northwest, which I didn't really mind. It was better than the snow we had left in Moab, and I was used to overcast skies from living in northeastern Ohio.

While I was exploring, Robin called me and told me that Paul was upset because she hadn't gone to see him to work things out. She asked me about seeking a divorce attorney and wanted to know what to do. I told her that if she was serious, getting a divorce attorney was a smart idea.

With all of this talk about a divorce attorney and how well we had connected in Moab, I started to think that Robin really did care about me. However, it was just a way for me to rationalize being with her and to pretend it wasn't an unhealthy situation. It was nice to feel wanted and needed, even if it was an illusion. Also, I was going to meet her son. *That has to mean something, right?*

A few hours later, I headed back to the beach house and waited for Robin's arrival. The nervousness I felt about meeting Robin's son wasn't unusual—meeting the child of someone you've just started "dating" for the first time can be a little nerve-wracking. I'm usually fine in such situations though, because the kids are normally too young to understand who I am and I don't actually spend every day with them. Robin's son, however, was nine, and he was really smart. Plus, I would be with living in the same house with him for a whole week.

When Robin's kid opened the door I didn't want some stranger's face to be the first thing he saw, so I hid out on the balcony looking over Fern Ridge Lake. I wanted them to get settled before he met some weird guy their mom had brought home. I figured he was going to have some apprehension about meeting me, considering I was a new guy and he was old enough to understand what was going on between his mother and me. I assumed this would all be strange for him, especially since he knew Paul and liked him, as everyone else did. I understood that kids that age are impressionable and I didn't want to be an adult he didn't like or resented. I decided I would treat him how I would have wanted to be treated at that age. I'd let him be the one to dictate how the week would go, and I would just be nice, hang out, and follow his lead.

When I heard the rocks crunch as Robin's car pulled into the driveway, the thought of just leaving crossed my mind, but I was in too deep now. After I gave them time to get settled, I went inside from the balcony to greet them. Her son was pretty standoffish. I wasn't Paul or his dad, and he let me know that immediately. I understood where he were coming from, so I made sure I didn't try to force him to like me or hang out with me. I let him warm up to me by just being nice and answering his questions.

He eventually grew to like me—well, as much as kids that age can. I actually spent far more time with him than I thought I would during the course of the week. Robin spent a lot of her time working in the living room, while he and I watched reality TV in the den or played games. Once he became more comfortable with me, he actually wanted to spend time with me, asked me to do things with him, and he was interested in what I thought. Sometimes he would grab me by the hand and drag me over to show me a picture he'd colored and he even fell asleep on my shoulder one time. Through this, I got a small glimpse of what it would be like to be a father, and I liked it. I even thought I could be a great dad, despite the fact I'd grown up without the best role models.

During the course of the week, we went out on the town a few times and had dinner and drinks and met up with Robin's friends who lived in Eugene. Back at the house, we would be together every night. Downstairs, right outside mine and Robin's room and just beyond the spiral staircase, was a door that led outside to a covered porch under a balcony. This was where Robin and I would escape and have our secret talks about us and our future.

The day before everyone was to arrive, Robin spent that entire afternoon on the phone and texting. I assumed she was talking to Paul, because that night, when I leaned over to kiss her, she stopped me and said, "Not tonight."

The next day was Thanksgiving which meant about a dozen of Robin's friends would be over. I, Robin, and her kid went shopping together at Whole Foods. We split up the items on our list and bought accordingly. As we were shopping, Robin dropped a bomb on me. Not only were a bunch of her friends and their kids coming over for Thanksgiving, but she had also invited Nick from Moab to join us.

"Why would you do that?" I asked, upset.

"Why not? He's harmless," she insisted.

I think she liked the fact that he liked her and maybe wanted to see me squirm or see how I would react. I was pissed because it meant I was going to have to watch him the entire time, nervous about his feelings toward Robin, and I didn't trust her either. It was like I was trading places with Paul again and had to worry about someone else hooking up with Robin. What could I do, though? He was coming.

In reality, the situation was all of my own creation. My insecurities and low self-esteem were coming out, along with my lack of faith in Robin. It was becoming evident that she didn't care about my feelings as much as I cared about hers, although this should have been clear to me months ago.

In preparation for the Friendsgiving festivities, her son wanted to make cheesecake from scratch. Robin had enough on her plate with the rest of the food preparations, so I told him I would make it with him. I had never made cheesecake from scratch before. Hell, I'd never made anything from scratch before, but I figured I could just follow a recipe. I wanted her son to be heavily involved since it was his project, so we researched recipes online together, and picked out one he wanted to make.

It was fun creating something from nothing, and making cheesecake with Robin's kid was challenging enough that we all felt a sense of accomplishment when it was done. He would argue with me over who got to mix cream cheese and sugar together or the graham crackers and butter for the crust. There was a minor debate about who was in charge of the topping, so I relented and let him do most of the work. It all came together in the end. Her son did give me something of a hard time, telling me that Paul was a better cook, and he would have done a better job, but I took it all in stride. It was a good bonding experience, and by the end of it, he seemed to genuinely be my friend. Even better, the cheesecake was a smashing success.

Once everyone started arriving for dinner, I knew it was going to be a weird Friendsgiving. Robin had told her friends not to take any pictures because she didn't want Paul to see them on social media. They abided by this, so I assume it was a normal request from her, since they didn't seem to question it. I didn't feel good about it, though. I thought it was bullshit. If I wanted to put my values and dignity aside to be with her, this was the type of nonsense I would need to put up with. Of course, in my heart, I was hoping someone would take pictures anyway and post them. I didn't necessarily want Paul to see them, I just didn't want Robin to dictate who was allowed to share their own pictures and experiences. Strangely, it was Nick who came through in violating Robin's rule. Although I wasn't a fan of him, he did manage to take a few pictures and put them up on his Instagram. I never heard anything about Paul's seeing them.

Nick wasn't able to drive because of some legal issues, so he'd taken the Greyhound bus from Portland. This seemed silly to me because he had his own family who he now wouldn't be spending Thanksgiving with. It felt like he was trying too hard. He also knew that Robin and I were in a "relationship" because he had sent us a message on social media when we posted our relationship status on Facebook the week before, congratulating us and telling us he couldn't have been happier.

I suspected he had ulterior motives, so to prevent a full shit-show disaster, I offered to pick him up from the bus station. I was going with the old philosophy of "Keep your friends close and your enemies closer." When I picked him up, he had his dog with him.

"You were allowed to bring your dog on the bus?" I asked, confused.

"Not usually, but I lied and said he was a service dog and I needed him to function," he replied, proud of his deceit.

This was the caliber of person I was dealing with. I asked him when he was leaving, and he said the next day. That was a relief, at least.

Once at the house Nick hit on Robin constantly. He was always by her side. No matter where she went, he would follow her around like a puppy, making sure he was sitting or standing next to her. This was not the way to earn Robin's affection, though. I tried to tell him to lay off, but he just ignored me and carried on. My blood started to boil and I was on the verge of wanting to punch him in the face. Then I thought, *This must be exactly how Paul felt with me in Tahoe in the parking lot.* I thought better of resorting to physical violence and tried to wait out the situation.

Despite Nick, I had a blast for the most part. Soon people started leaving and eventually, it was only me, Robin, her kid, and Nick. He was staying the night. Nick was out on the balcony alone while Robin was putting her son to bed and I took this opportunity to have a one-on-one chat with him.

"You know Robin is my girlfriend, right?" I asked, not really having a better description for our dysfunctional relationship status.

"Yeah, I know, man," he said.

"Then lay off, dude," I told him.

I thought he'd gotten the message, but I didn't have time to follow up because Robin walked out on the balcony and told Nick that he could sleep on the couch upstairs and that she and I were going to bed downstairs together. And to my relief he agreed.

The next morning, Robin was planning on going on a hike with her friends and their kids, so it fell to me to take Nick back to the bus station. He, however, had other plans. He wanted to stay longer.

We later learned that earlier in the morning, Nick got up, stole a boat from the shared boat storage next to our house down by the beach, and went out on the water. This was odd for several reasons: 1) he didn't tell anyone he was doing this; 2) he stole a boat he knew wasn't ours to use; 3) he left his dog at the house for us to watch; and 4) he had to catch a bus in a few hours. Making matters worse, as he was stealing the boat, he managed to accidentally release another boat in the water, which floated away. It seemed as if he was looking for an excuse to miss his bus ride home.

Robin was furious. I had never seen her this upset before. Nick was way out on the water, we couldn't communicate with him, and we had to recover the boat that had floated away. I stole another boat to retrieve the drifting one, and Nick eventually made it back. When he did, Robin ripped into him. "You're a fucking asshole. Those aren't our boats. We could get into serious trouble."

Nick claimed he didn't realize he wasn't allowed to take the boat and that he just wanted to stay with us for a few more days. But Robin wasn't having any more of his bullshit. She was finally seeing through his charade, so she lied and said we needed to be out of the house that day, when we really had a few more days left.

With that, Robin left for her hike with her friends and told me that she wanted Nick gone by the time she got back. I countered that I hadn't wanted him there in the first place. As soon as she left, I told Nick to get his shit together because we were going to the bus station. I didn't care what time his bus was leaving; I wanted him gone. He gathered his belongings, and I dropped him off. As I drove back, I was relieved, but I was afraid that he would just show up back at the house. Maybe this was the way Paul felt about me. Luckily, that was the last time I saw Nick.

The next few days were uneventful. Robin was distant, and I knew our relationship and our time together were coming to an end. She needed to get back to Tahoe to figure out her life. We still went out to dinner and to bookstores together, but the spark between us seemed to have gone. Robin was ready to drop her kid off and finish this adventure. I wanted it to last longer, preferably until she saw the light and wanted to be with me. Not because I knew she really cared about me, but because I didn't want to go back to my own reality.

In the end, Robin decided to leave the house a day before our rental term was up. I tried to convince her to stay, but it was to no avail. She encouraged me to stay the extra day, and I took her up on it. I had paid half for the place anyhow, and I wanted to stay. I didn't know what I was going to do with my life just yet. Yes, I needed to get back to Ohio sometime, but that's all I knew.

The morning Robin left there was no big farewell, but I knew this was my last taste of the Robin adventure. I helped her load up her car and said goodbye to her kid, although he didn't seem to care. Then I said goodbye to Robin. I told her this was probably the last time I would ever see her and that I wished it wasn't. She insisted it wasn't going to be the last time, but we both knew the truth. We kissed goodbye, and then she was gone.

I was alone without Robin for the first time in about a month. That evening, I had an IPA, watched some Netflix, and went to bed. I thought about going to see other friends in the area whom I had met while I was on my adventures, but they were all busy and unable to hang out until next week and I didn't want to wait around.

The next day, I bade farewell to the beach house and started my drive back to Ohio. This drive was different from all the others. Winter was here, and there was snow for most of my drive. The season had come to an end, just like my relationship with Robin.

CHAPTER 12
GOING ULTRA
FORWARD GROWTH

In the winter of 2013, Pope Francis had moved into the Vatican, and I was about to move back to Ohio from NYC. A few months before the move, I was packing up boxes when I glanced toward the full-length mirror leaning up against the wall in my studio apartment. The person looking back at me was an overweight, out-of-shape guy with a promising double chin. I had ballooned to over two hundred pounds, and I am about five foot ten on a good day.

When I was a kid and teenager, I never really had a problem with my weight. I certainly never considered myself fat. I had a great metabolism and was very active in sports, running around the neighborhood, and skateboarding. It wasn't until I hit college that I started putting on a few pounds. In college, I wasn't exercising at all, and I was drinking a lot and eating whatever I wanted, whenever I wanted. Working at Swensons didn't help either; I had too many double cheeseburgers every shift. After college, I didn't change my diet too much. I didn't think I was fat; I just thought I had to lose a few pounds. It was nothing to be concerned about for me. The truth was, I was clinically obese. When I moved out to San Francisco, I was more active and the pounds came off without my even trying, though I was still overweight. Then, when I was in law school, I put the weight back on. Studying constantly, a sedentary lifestyle, and a lack of exercise didn't exactly do wonders for my health. When I moved out to New York City, I put on even more weight because I was working constantly, stressing out, not exercising often, going out drinking, and still eating whatever I wanted. So when I saw myself in the mirror that day, I knew this was an issue I needed to address before I moved back to Ohio.

To be honest, I didn't know how to address my weight. I had dabbled in running a little bit in San Francisco and in law school, but nothing serious. Also, by the time I was about to move back to Ohio, I had already run two marathons: the Philadelphia Marathon with Gary and a few years before that, the New York City Marathon with my sister. I used these two marathons to "prove" that I was in shape. In reality, they just enabled me to continue lying to myself. I ran both of these marathons out of shape with dismal times. But on that life-changing morning, the mirror didn't lie.

I started running because I wanted to get in shape and because I loved the feeling of being outdoors, exploring, and challenging myself. Running is good exercise, but it didn't necessarily mean I was going to lose weight. When I was training for my first two marathons, I would use my training runs as an excuse to eat a lot. I didn't understand why I wasn't losing any weight. In fact, I was gaining weight.

The night of the mirror incident, after I ate a few frozen chicken burritos and several chocolate chip cookies, I watched a documentary entitled *Forks over Knives*. This documentary advocated a whole-foods, plant-based diet. I ate up everything the movie said, both literally and figuratively. People featured in the movie had lost weight and gotten healthy almost instantly after adopting a plant-based diet. I was so moved by the movie, I haven't eaten a piece of meat since. When I coupled this diet with running, the weight came off even when I wasn't trying to lose it.

That summer, I packed up a rented minivan and headed west to Columbus, Ohio, where my sister lived. I had never lived in Columbus, even though it was two hours south of my hometown, Cuyahoga Falls. I didn't want to move back there because it had too many bad influences and bad memories for me. Plus, I wanted to experience something different. For the fifth time in my life, I rented an apartment sight unseen and moved without a job.

When I arrived, I went crazy applying for jobs, but nothing came to fruition. I wanted something more than working at Applebee's; I was a licensed attorney for goodness' sake. I was starting to become depressed and scared that I had made a huge mistake in moving back to Ohio. I was on the verge of running out of my unemployment benefits and I felt worthless. I had literally no income and bills to pay.

Finally, I received a job offer as a legal recruiter. It was a job I would soon come to despise in a miserable, cutthroat environment. It was the opposite of what I was used to at Gary's company. I knew how to play the game though and could be a savvy salesperson if I wanted to. It paid the bills, but it didn't make me feel good about myself when I went home at the end of the day.

In hindsight, I'm glad I hated that job so much because while I was working there I decided to start my own continuing education company, like the one I had worked at with Gary. I thought, *If Gary can be successful with this, why couldn't I?* I knew the business very well, and it didn't take much capital to get started, which was appealing because I didn't have any money.

After work each day, I went straight to the library to work on my new business. I watched YouTube videos for hours about how to create a paid membership-based website. Once that was up and running, I needed content. I had done a few programs while I worked with Gary, so I decided, because I am a lawyer, I could just record my own content for the time being. Once I got going, I could recruit other professionals to provide additional material.

Then I went through the process of getting the course accredited in Ohio so professionals would be able to receive credit for it. Once the course was approved, I put it live on my website. Within an hour, I got my first sale. *Holy shit!* I wasn't even advertising yet. Hell, I wasn't even really ready yet. I had a sale though, a sale from something I had created out of nothing. It was amazing and it only reinforced my belief that I could make this work. Then I thought, *If this first program is successful, why don't I expand to other states?* So that's what I did.

After four months as a legal recruiter, I quit and focused solely on my own business. I probably didn't quit in the most professional way. My boss worked in Minnesota, and I wrote her an email about how I couldn't work in this environment anymore. Then I told one of my work colleagues, whom I didn't get along with, that I was going to grab a cup of coffee—and I never went back.

I also didn't tell Gary, at first, about starting my own business. I thought he might be upset that I was "stealing" his idea. I got a call from him one day and he didn't seem happy, and I knew the jig was up. He told me that he just wished he hadn't heard about it from someone else. He also told me something I'll never forget: "I can't be angry or upset with you because that would speak more to insecurities about me and my company. I wish you all the best." So with his "blessing" and our friendship still intact, I was on my way with this new venture.

I decided now to move to Cleveland. My sister had her own life and friends in Columbus and I didn't really feel a part of it. Also, Triple B and my mom were moving closer to Columbus, and I didn't want to be around when that happened. I had a few friends up in Cleveland, and I could do my new job from anywhere, so I moved once again.

In Cleveland, I spent a lot of time alone. I didn't really hang out with my friends because they spent most of their time drinking and smoking weed, so I had no choice but to focus on my business, and it grew as a result.

I also started a regular meditation practice at this time, because so many people I admired swore by it. It quieted my mind and helped me gain clarity and focus, both of which I needed. Also, it was a good tool to keep panic attacks at bay. At this time, I started to gravitate toward a new group of friends, too: trail runners. I wanted to stay fit and be around people who would push my limits. I joined a local running group and slowly stopped spending time with my old friends.

As I got more and more into running, I spent a lot of time reading about the subject, especially ultra-marathon runners. There was something about ultra-running that was exciting and fascinating. It seemed like a challenge of the mind and body. I liked the idea of being stripped down to nothing emotionally and seeing what I was really capable of. When my body is telling me to quit at mile forty because I feel like my legs or body can't move, it's my mind that I use to convince me otherwise—if I'm strong enough to convince myself—and that's what makes ultra-marathon running the ultimate mental challenge. I run because I like to push my own boundaries, see what's on the other side of fear, and know what I'm truly capable of. I felt that if I could run a hundred miles without stopping, there wasn't anything in this world I couldn't do. At the same time, I'm sure my somewhat addictive personality liked the idea of the races and running. It was something I could be obsessed with that had a—mostly—positive impact.

I was also inspired by Dean Karnazes's book *Ultramarathon Man* and Christopher McDougall's book *Born to Run*, both of which are about the sport of ultra-running.

In addition, I discovered that some of the best ultra-runners don't eat meat. I read Scott Jurek's book *Eat and Run* and Rich Roll's book *Finding Ultra*. They're both ultra-endurance athletes who are also vegan. Scott Jurek is arguably one of the best ultra-runners ever. He has won the most prestigious ultra-marathon in the United States, the Western States 100, seven times in a row. Rich Roll is a recovering alcoholic who got into races later in life. When Rich was in his forties, he completed the Epic 5—five ultra-ironman-distances in less than a week. Both of these guys inspired me because they are normal humans who dedicated themselves to something and made it work; there is nothing sensational about them besides their athletic endurance achievements, and I was able to relate and believe I was capable of more. If they could do it, so could I.

I was getting in better shape and dropped from 200 pounds to under 160. Inspired by the books I had read and ready for my next challenge, I signed up for an ultra-marathon in Washington, DC—The North Face Endurance Challenge fifty-mile trail race—on June 6, 2014. I fully intended to dedicate my mind and body to accomplishing this goal. I needed to see what I was capable of.

I'm not the fastest runner, and I didn't run track in high school or college. I did run in junior high though, where I did the hurdles, the 800-meters, and the long jump, and I was pretty good at all of them. So with this extensive running background, I was ready to tackle the ultra-marathon distance.

Now I just needed a plan. And not only did I need a plan, but I needed to follow through with it. I researched online training programs for a fifty-mile race. I also knew that nutrition was a big part of training, and I was determined to use my new secret of plant power for the race.

I had never done a trail race, let alone a fifty-miler, and I didn't know what to expect. I decided to volunteer at another fifty-miler to see what I was going to be in for. The North Face holds trail races throughout the year and throughout the world, so finding one of their races to volunteer at wasn't difficult. I found one in Bear Mountain, New York, which was about an hour north of New York City. My job was to man an aid station and help runners refuel at about twenty-two miles in.

Volunteering at the race turned out to provide crucial information. As runners came into the aid station, grabbed a quick bite, and filled their hydration packs as fast as they could, I soaked up information like a sponge. I made sure to take notice of what they were wearing, how they ate, how much time they spent at the station, and even how they ran. This was all foreign to me, and I fell in love with it instantly. I knew I wanted to experience being on the other side of the aid station.

During the race, I saw the fastest trail runners in the world and others who were basically just walking. Some runners even had pacers to keep them company and encourage them.

If I was going to attempt something this epic, I was going to need to have someone just as epic as a pacer for my first time.

Enter Joseph from my old company in NYC.

Joseph was an accomplished marathon runner, and I knew I would benefit so much from his company and experience during the race.

In the days leading up to the race, I was confident that I had done everything in my power to prepare as much as possible. I drove to Algonkian Regional Park in Sterling, Virginia—where the race would actually take place—a day early to check things out and get settled in. I went down to the starting line and watched the volunteers setting up tents and preparing for the next day's event. I picked Joseph up from the train station, and we went to an information session in Georgetown for a pre-race report and talk being held by the race organizers. I needed to get as much information as possible.

When we arrived, though, I was surprised by how few people were there. The race was the next day, and there were thousands signed up to run different distances: the marathon, fifty kilometers, relay team, or fifty-miles. The information was interesting but not crucial. They let us know how our "bibs" were going to be marked by officials as we made our way through the various loops around the course. Still, it was helpful from a mental aspect to know what to expect the next day so I wasn't left wondering and I felt more prepared.

After the meeting, I dropped Joseph off at the hotel. I wouldn't see him again until mile thirty during the race, where he would start running with me. I had an early dinner and tried to get some sleep. I needed to be up for a five a.m. race start.

The next morning, the hotel gave me a three a.m. wake-up call, and I rolled out of bed, excited. I was pleasantly surprised that I had actually gotten a good night's sleep, considering what was ahead of me. I had already laid all of my clothes and supplies out the night before, so now I donned my gray shorts and blue shirt. I pinned my race bib on my shorts. I filled my handheld water bottle with a mix of grape Gatorade and water. Then I stuffed as many gels in the available pockets as I could. For breakfast, I feasted on a banana and an everything bagel with almond butter. The race was only about four miles from my hotel, but I headed down early because I knew my nerves would send me to the port-a-potty a few times. I just wanted to get this thing going. I had dedicated almost six months of my life to preparing for this moment, and now it was here.

This race was divided into different "waves" and times, so as to not clog up the trail with all the runners in the first few miles of the race. Different distances would also start at different times. Most ultras don't have waves for the same distance but this was an event with The North Face which attracted a higher number of runners. Usually, the faster runners, or "elites," are in the first wave. Ultrarunning is one of the few sports where amateurs are able to compete toe-to-toe with the elites, and though I was originally selected to be in wave two, I had the option of moving up to wave one. I wanted a good start and to know what it felt like to start a race with the fastest runners, so I went with wave one.

Dean Karnazes, the Ultramarathon Man, was there to start us off, but he wasn't running. Dean raised the starter pistol toward sky, fired, and we were off. It was still dark out, and most of the runners wore headlamps. The sea of headlamps bobbing up and down through the forest was a strange and awe-inspiring sight. As soon as the race started, a group of four runners sprinted out from the first wave in front of everyone. *There's no way they can keep up that pace*, I thought. It was probably just a mind game on their end, which I suppose is something of a strategy.

I knew this was going to be a long day and there was no need to go out guns blazing so I stayed with the second group of the first wave, right behind the lead sprinters. The early miles took us along the edge of a pond where there was a thin layer of mist resting on top. At that moment, I didn't want to be anywhere else. I had this feeling of belonging, and I didn't want it to go away. All of these runners were here to run together in the woods. It was one of the best feelings in my life, and at that moment, I knew ultra-running was for me.

The group I was running with stuck together for the first ten or so miles. We saw the sun come up together as we followed each other along the single-track trail. As we ran, we would help each other out, and if there was a log or rock in the way, I'd hear the pack leader yell, "*Log!*" I had never experienced this type of camaraderie in a race before. It wasn't about competition; it was about the experience and making sure everyone finished the race. We had all done the training, and we were all in this together. We took turns leading the group, and I had my own chance to yell out *"Log!"* a few times. It felt good to keep tempo with a group.

Everything seemed to be going well—and then my first spot of trouble hit. Around mile eight, there was a small creek we were supposed to run though. As we approached the water, we were forced to stop. A huge tree had fallen and was blocking our path, and it was difficult to determine exactly how we were going to navigate it. Knowing that this was a race, I wanted to get by it as quickly as possible, so I decided to jump over it. I climbed up on to the trunk and jumped off landing hard on my right leg. As soon as I landed, I realized something didn't feel right and I was in immediate pain.

When I was a teenager, I had torn my ACL while playing backyard football. I'd never had surgery to fix it, just rehab. Now I had reinjured that knee jumping off the tree. It hurt and was bruised, but I was determined to go on; I hadn't trained this hard to give up now. I took a few aspirin and tried to push the pain out of my mind. I couldn't quit anyhow, not with Joseph waiting for me.

I managed to stay with the group I had started with until mile thirteen. At that point, some of them fell behind and a few pulled ahead. By then, the sun was high above us, and it was getting warmer. I still felt great but there was a long way to go. There was also a lot of talking going on between the runners, and I wasn't in the mood to talk—I needed as much energy for running as possible. Although it was nice to listen to others' conversations to keep my mind off the pain I was experiencing.

When we headed into Great Falls—one of the checkpoints around mile fifteen—an official shouted out our current placings and as I passed him, he screamed, "Twelfth place, keep it up." I was floored. I knew it was still early in the race, but I was ecstatic and a smile came across my face. *I can do this. I can do really well*, I thought.

There was also an aid station at Great Falls with drop bags, and I saw two runners ahead of me stop. I passed them, climbing to tenth place. It was time to put my head down and focus on meeting up with Joseph.

By the time I reached him, I was still in the top fifteen or so. He started running, clearly expecting us to be going a lot faster than we were, but I was hurting. At this stage, too, I saw a few elite runners who had gone out with the first group sitting down at the aid station. I thought it was weird that I had caught up with them. I later learned that they ended up dropping out and I used it as motivation to keep going.

Eventually, the heat, my exhaustion, and my lack of experience got the better of me. I started walking and slipped out of the top fifteen. By then, I didn't really care. I just wanted the race to be over.

The last thirteen miles were the hardest miles I had ever run. I ran out of fluids, and it got to the point where my urine was very dark—not a good sign. Then my knee really started hurting, and I had to question whether I could complete the race. I fell four times but took more aspirin and kept moving. My body wasn't prepared for this heat, and it was hard to stay hydrated.

In the last ten miles, I was passed seven times. I managed to run the last few miles and ended up in twenty-fourth place. I was in the top twenty-five and had finished in under nine hours! Not bad for my first fifty-mile trail race. There were many times when I wanted to quit, but because of Joseph, my training, and my mental toughness, I made it.

The feeling of finishing that trail race in the top twenty-five was incredible. It boosted my confidence no end. A big part of that confidence came from knowing that this wasn't just a local trail race. This was put on by the North Face and had brought in some elite athletes. Now, all I wanted to do was run trail races and be around the trail-running tribe constantly. All of my training and the meatless diet had paid off. If I could dial both of those up even more, I was sure that the sky was the limit of what I was capable of.

Northeast Ohio, surprisingly, has an incredible trail running scene. Home to Cuyahoga Valley National Park with, seemingly, endless miles of single track running trails to explore. Although I did find a great group of trail runners in Cleveland and ran with them for the next few years, competing in many more ultras and even winning a 50K, they didn't live and breathe ultra-running like I craved. They also had families and jobs that took up most of their time. I wanted to challenge myself not only physically, but also mentally. I wanted to become everything I knew I was capable of. I didn't think I was going to find what I was searching for, or the tribe I was looking for, in Ohio. All the best trail races and runners were out west. This was one of the reasons why I decided to buy a van and travel west. I didn't realize I wasn't ready for what was waiting for me there.

CHAPTER 13
GOODBYE
I THINK I'M ALONE NOW

Over five months had passed since the day I bought the van and traveled to the Pacific Northwest, Tahoe, Moab, and beyond. It was now late 2016. To everyone's surprise, Donald Trump was the president-elect of the United States, and to my surprise, I was making my way back to Cleveland from Eugene after spending Thanksgiving with Robin and her kid. I had started this adventure in late July, and it was now December. Although I had traveled back to Ohio a few times over the course of my adventure, it felt like I had been gone the entire time.

I had the unmistakable feeling that I might not be going back west any time soon, or at least, I wouldn't be going back in the van. I was also pretty confident that I would never see Robin again, though we were still in constant contact. I'd had the same feeling about not seeing Robin again after I left her in Washington. Same with Tahoe. So I really wasn't sure. The drive back east on I-80 was very different from when I had first set out in late July, when the sun was shining and there was a world of possibilities ahead of me. Now, in early December, it was colder and the gray clouds and sporadic snowfall harried my drive.

Once I arrived in Ohio, I tried to get back into something of a routine and figure out what my next move would be. I still couldn't run because my knee was fucked up, and I was out of shape. I had fallen in love with the west and decided that I didn't want to live in Ohio anymore. I started to think about moving west and figuring things out when I got there. There was nothing in Ohio for me: my job didn't keep me there, I didn't have a significant other to stay for, I didn't have any kids, and I didn't have many real friends to speak of. *If I could live anywhere, why am I choosing here?* I thought. What I hadn't yet realized was that I was going to be a shit show no matter where I went. That wouldn't change until I faced my demons.

Via text, I told Robin how I was going to move out west and that she should come live with me. We even talked about getting a place together in Oregon, though I was more into the idea than she was. Even if we couldn't live together, perhaps we could live in the same city. She said she was going to move from Tahoe and almost leased a home in Bend, Oregon.

It seemed like Robin and I were communicating more now than we ever did when we were physically together. She would text me that she missed me, and there were even a few times when she told me she loved me. Even though there were thousands of miles and her marriage between us, I thought there was a possibility of our being together one day.

But she just couldn't let go of Paul. I had the feeling that she was never going to let him go. Still, we texted and pretended we would be together soon. I had gotten good at pretending that things I wished to be true were.

But then I was used to pretending—that was how I had been raised. My mom wanted to believe we were the perfect family, so she pretended that's what we were, just as she pretended that she had selected the perfect husband. I believe she was too embarrassed and ashamed to admit her mistake and that it was easier for her to just pretend. Maybe she wasn't strong enough or didn't think she deserved better. That's certainly what I thought, so that's what I did most of my life—pretend.

I had pretended that I wasn't raised by an abusive stepfather. I had pretended that I could be happy if I skipped over what hurt most inside. And now I was pretending that Robin was the right person for me and that we could make it work. Pretending seemed easier than confronting reality. Until I couldn't pretend anymore.

Over the course of the next few weeks, Robin finally confided to me that she didn't really feel like she was capable of love. This didn't shock me, given the way she would rarely show her feelings. I didn't bring up the fact that she had already told me she loved me. I believe she was trying to prepare me so that I wouldn't be crushed when she finally told me there wasn't a future for us together.

Everything—from how she was acting to what she was telling me—should have been a deal-breaker. But I just couldn't face this; I didn't have enough self-worth or self-esteem or self-confidence. I was still in love with the idea of her, so I kept gravitating back toward her, no matter what she said. Maybe I thought she was my ticket and my reason to move out west. I knew in my heart that we wouldn't be together forever, but she did represent a whole new life for me.

Then everything changed with one text conversation:
Robin: FUCK. You were totally wrong
Me: About?

Robin: What's the worst possible thing?
Me: You're staying with Paul?
Robin: No. I'm over a week late. So I took a test and it's positive. Hopefully it's wrong.
Me: Oh shit.

She sent me a picture of the positive pregnancy test, and I just stared at it in disbelief and shock. I had no reason to believe she would make this up and as far as I knew she was pregnant with my child.

I shouldn't have been all that surprised; we hadn't used protection at all during our affair. And now Robin was pregnant with my child—my child! For the first time in my life, I wasn't going to just be pretending for myself; there was going to be someone else in the picture.

I wasn't sure what to make of it all. It was easy to say hypothetically what I would do if the situation ever came up, but now it had actually happened, so many thoughts raced through my head, I didn't know which one to follow: *Looks like I'm going to be a father. Should I be a father? Can I be a father? Maybe she shouldn't have the baby. She has to have the baby. Where will this baby live? Does this mean Robin and I will get married? What will Paul think? Shit, what about Paul? Will I need to fight for my right to this child?* Making matters more difficult was the fact that she was over two thousand miles away.

She soon sent me a picture of a second pregnancy test, which digitally proclaimed: "PREGNANT."

Shit, I thought again. *Now what?*

I needed to do the responsible thing first. Robin was also upset and scared, and I desperately wanted to reassure her that we would figure things out. I tried to call her, but she didn't pick up. Instead, she texted me and said she didn't want to talk right now. We agreed to have a phone conversation the next day.

"What do you want to do?" Robin asked, concern clear in her voice even over the phone.

"Listen, I will support any decision you make and will be there for you no matter what. However, I would rather have the child," I said surprisingly calmly.

"It's hard. It means making some seriously long-term plans. If I didn't love you so much, I wouldn't even be having this discussion at all. And I love the idea of having a family with you, Kyle. I think you'd be an awesome dad. I feel more secure in a relationship with you than anyone I've had a relationship with in recent history," she said. I was thinking to myself that she'd recently told me she wasn't capable of love. But I just focused on what I wanted to hear.

"You should embrace that." I was trying to convince her and myself that we should do this.

However, I already knew where she was going with her decision. I had known from the moment she told me she was pregnant. She wasn't going to go through with the pregnancy. After all, she was married and didn't feel like she had time to raise another child. She'd confided before that she wasn't ready to go through having a baby again. For the second time during this adventure I was getting stung, but it wasn't the yellow jackets from Loon Lake this time, it was my heart bearing the brunt of the attack from Robin's words.

I understood her reasons and even told her I would take care of the child the majority of the time. But I knew deep down that having a child with Robin wouldn't be a good idea. At that point, I think I just wanted to have some sort of relationship with or attachment to her, which is not the best reason to have a kid. I also had the thought that I wasn't getting any younger and that this might be my only opportunity to have a child. But it wasn't Robin's responsibility to make me a father—it wasn't fair to put that pressure on her.

After a lot of back-and-forth, it was decided that she would not have the baby. I didn't know the details about how the procedure worked or if there even was a procedure. I asked her if she wanted me to fly out there and go to the doctor with her, but she didn't want me there. She also needed to sneak off and get this done without Paul knowing. I supported her in this decision, though I wasn't happy about it and sent her half of the money.

As it got closer to Christmas, I was in a daze. I wasn't sure how to cope with the sudden discovery and then loss of my child. I wasn't mad at Robin. In fact, I still missed being around her. I missed being out west. Robin and I had spent most of our time attached at the hip ever since we'd met. But if I really thought about it, did I miss being around her or did I just miss the adventure?

Back in my gloomy apartment, I spent days looking for places to live in Oregon and was convinced I was going to move there in the near future. I kept telling everyone around me that I was moving out west. I wanted Robin to know that I'd be closer to her soon. I kept thinking, *If I had been closer, she would have had the child*. I wanted her to wait for me, and she kept my interest and excitement by sending me text messages. I would text back because I liked the attention and I wanted her in my life. We even exchanged Christmas gifts through the mail. But in my heart, I didn't feel right about the situation.

New Year's Eve came and went, and I was still texting with Robin all night. I lied to her about going out and having fun with friends that night, when I was really just alone in my apartment, trying to sleep. With her, I always wanted to appear to be fun and busy. I didn't want her to think that I wasn't interesting or didn't have other things going on in my life. I was just trying to keep her attention. I was sure that if I told her she was all I thought about, I'd lose her, because that would mean she already had me. She never liked it when things came too easily.

The loss of the baby had unexpected emotional consequences for me. I don't want to say it was the wrong decision, but it definitely messed me up for a while. I was sad and angry all at once. I started drinking a lot and tried to hook up with random girls I didn't know. I was contacting my ex-girlfriends, asking if they wanted to hang out. I even messaged one of my friends' girlfriends who I knew liked me and met her at a bar. We ended up making out. My friend eventually found out anyway, and our relationship suffered because of it. I wasn't in a good place and was just looking for an outlet.

Robin wasn't in a good place, either. I can't even imagine what she was going through. She would text or call me constantly, sometimes upset, sometimes happy. She was all over the place.

I was sure now that Robin and I were never going to be together. We might never even see each other again. I still thought I was going to live out west—even if it was going to be away from her and on my own terms. I thought I belonged out there, and I was determined to go. Then I got a long text from Robin:

> *It's official, I'm staying with Paul. I do want to say that I'm sorry that everything worked out in such a way that we may not get to hang out, even as friends. I feel that is*

> *a loss for both of us, and it sucks. I am doing the best I can to make the choices I need to make in my life right now. I think in hindsight it would've been in our best interest not to have all the drama we had. I don't regret hanging out with you or any of that part I only regret our unfortunate decision to post a relationship status on Facebook that was still very undeveloped and relatively new. That's a tough way to get going...*

She was right. Although I thought her decision to stay with Paul was a bad one, but I couldn't talk her out of it. She never listened to me in these types of situations. I believed it wasn't going to turn out well for them. If I was honest, though, I knew that if I had had the option to be with her, that would have been a bad decision too.

It was something of a relief to have all of the Robin drama over. It wasn't what I wanted in my life or what I thought about when I imagined the girl I wanted to be with. I loved being with her because her life was an adventure and she took me along on that adventure. I wanted that in my life; I craved it. But the adventure was not what it seemed from the outside. When I jumped on that train, it was a very different experience to what I expected. Still, I wouldn't have changed it for anything.

I needed to look at my time with Robin and see what it said about me. Why was I so hell-bent on being with her when I knew in my heart the relationship wasn't good for me? Was I attracted to the drama? To traumatic, unhealthy relationships? Didn't I think I deserved better? Why was I so afraid of being alone?

I looked inside myself. I looked at my past and what I had been through. It all seemed to come down to one thing that I had always tried to pretend away: the fact that I had been abused as a child. The fear and uncertainty that I grew up with stayed with me throughout adulthood. I needed to face myself without shame or embarrassment so I could move on.

Despite all the flaws in our relationship, Robin was one of the most amazing people I had ever met. She knew exactly what she wanted out of life and went for it. I still dream of having that kind of courage. Robin taught me so much, not only about ultra-running and the outdoors, but about myself and what I really wanted out of life. I hope, too, that she learned from our relationship as well. I believe we were both in a rough part of our lives, trying to figure things out and looking for an escape. It was a perfect storm.

Going on the van adventure was supposed to be my path to fulfillment. It was my way of saying that society's version of success is not mine and that I could do my own thing. I didn't realize it at the time, but it was also an attempt to escape my past without having to confront it. I had to confront what I had been through and recognize it for what it was. Then, and only then, could I find happiness and contentment. Evidently, for me to come to this realization, I just needed to go through an emotional wringer of my own making.

The pregnancy and adventure out west were all too much for me. I didn't know how to handle it or why it had all happened. The only thing I knew for sure was that I wasn't the same person anymore. I was frustrated with myself for having gone on this adventure and caused all this drama and carnage. It was like I was ruining people's lives, as well as my own. But what made me most upset was the fact that I still wasn't happy and I didn't seem to learn from my past. *What the fuck do I have to do?*

I needed to make some immediate changes. Starting with surrounding myself with people who cared about me and themselves.

I began writing about my adventure. I wanted to have some sort of record of what I'd experienced. Once I started writing, it made sense to start at the beginning, and for me, the beginning was when I was four years old and met Triple B. And once I opened the Pandora's box of my childhood and adolescence, I was finally able to realize and accept that I had been abused as a child. Abuse is such a loaded word and I hesitate to use it. But I need to call it out for what it was in order heal from the trauma. It was a jarring revelation for me to come to terms, in my late thirties, about what happened to me when I was growing up. I had never thought that I had been abused before—because I didn't want to admit it. It also seemed that I had regressed when I went out west and got mixed up in unhealthy relationships and activities—but I just wasn't ready yet to face who I was or what happened to me.

The emotional abuse I'd endured was far worse than the physical abuse, because the emotional abuse seems to have had a bigger impact on my life. In addition, because I had never dealt with the trauma, it was still continuing. All the pieces started coming together like a jigsaw puzzle; I was beginning to see the bigger picture. It all began to make sense: why I still felt so uncomfortable around Triple B, why I disliked going to see him, why I wanted to just leave whenever I was in his presence, why I had unhealthy relationships, why I was always searching for more, and on and on . . .

My mom had always wanted us to make an effort and pretend, and so I had pretended for her sake and because she is still married to Triple B. But now, I realized that I shouldn't have to hide my experience just to make her more comfortable. It was hurting and tearing me apart inside. I wasn't able to have healthy relationships with anyone, least of all myself. I love my mom so very much, but there had to come a point when I made my health and happiness paramount. Then, and only then, would I be able to heal and help others. Maybe even my mom.

My mom's argument was always in Triple B's defense: "Your father has done so much for you." Her calling Triple B my father made healing even harder. She was trying to force a narrative that wasn't there. But even if he had done all the things she claimed for me, it still wouldn't have made it okay for him to treat me the way he did. Instead of doing things for me, he could have told me he loved me. He could have told me he cared about me. He could have asked me about my day. He could have said he was sorry.

I was angry when I finally realized what I had experienced. Of course, I couldn't help but think how much better my life would have been if Triple B had never come into it. That's an easy rabbit hole to fall down. Once I started, I was filled with anger and rage, and I didn't want those feelings. So I needed to let them go. I needed to forgive so I could get on with my life and heal.

Just because I've forgiven him, it doesn't mean I need to have a meaningful relationship with him. If he wanted to change and take steps for us to have a relationship, I'd be all for it. But I can't force anyone to change. The forgiveness is only for myself. I want to live with love, not hate. Forgiveness is love, and that's all I want my life to be filled with: love for Triple B, love for Robin, love for my mom, love for myself, and love for everyone in my life.

I don't blame anyone. I know I have hurt people too and I am sorry for that. Every day, I try to be grateful for my life and I try to be a better person. I truly believe all of this needed to happen. I needed to have a disaster adventure out west. I even needed to meet Triple B. It all had to be, so I could see the truth of who I really am. All I ever really wanted was to love and to be loved.

CONCLUSION

It's been several years since I left the Fern Ridge Lake beach house. I miss it; I really do. I miss the adventure I was on, and I miss all the friends I made while I was on it. Of course, I miss Robin. Though as I now look back on my life and what has transpired, it is clear that I have changed. At the very least, I have a different perspective.

As I wrote this book, I struggled with *why* I was writing it. I didn't want to vilify anybody—not even Triple B or Robin. It wasn't about them. It was about me. *But what about me?* Just having a story to tell wasn't good enough for me or for the book. I wanted to share my experience and hoped that others would be able to gain something from it. I understand I come off as a jerk at moments, and more often than not I didn't learn from my mistakes—but I'm human. I wanted to be true to myself and the reader. Clearly, I in no way have it all figured out, and I was and still am trying to do the best I can.

I kept trying to escape and find happiness and meaning in new places and in toxic relationships or with drugs and alcohol, not knowing they wouldn't cure me. I kept trying to prove everyone wrong, and when I couldn't, I ended up unhappy. I needed to face myself and realize that if I just kept running away from what had happened to me, I would suffer the same fate for the rest of my life. The best way for me to come to terms with what I had been through and to heal was to share my story. I also needed to work on forgiving myself for all my mistakes to move forward—which is a work in progress, as is life.

I'm not upset with Robin. She made the best decisions for her at that time in her life and when we were together. I want nothing but the best for her. She is one of the most courageous and amazing women I have ever known.

I'm not upset with Triple B, either. He was raised in such a way that he didn't know how to be a father. I hope that someday he too comes to terms with what he went through and finds happiness. I'm always open to helping him with that.

Obviously, a huge tenet in my life has been to always keep pushing forward and not give up. But what I found was actually most important in my adventure—and in my life—was that the people I surrounded myself with ended up shaping my life, for better or for worse. I believe I am better off alone than with negative people. Success is subjective, and everyone needs to blaze their own path to happiness and fulfillment, not always go down the trail others tell them to follow— they need follow their own dragons and see where it leads.

I know now where I belong: wherever I am.

ACKNOWLEDGEMENTS

My sister, my brother, and my mom—I love you all more than you will ever know. I'm thankful each day you're in my life. Without the three of you, nothing else matters.

To the connection, Mary Kate, Wes, and the rest of my family, thank you for making me laugh on a daily basis and being there for me when I need you.

To my copy editor, Aja Pollack, this book wouldn't be anywhere close to readable without your talent for words and your keen eye. Lisa Bess Kramer and Kim Dinan, thank you for your initial feedback and thoughts on this book. They were crucial and helped me create the building blocks to form my words into a book. Andy Bridge, my cover designer, it was amazing how you brought to life exactly what I had envisioned in my mind. You were patient with me and I couldn't be happier with the finished product.

David Schnurman, you have impacted my life more than I can express with words. You gave me the strength and courage to believe in myself and go after what I want in life. I know this book wouldn't have existed if I'd never met you. Micah Bochart, you are everything I want to be as a human being. Thank you for giving me something to aspire to everyday. Frank Furbacher, Michele Richman, and Sigalle Barness—I couldn't have asked to work with better people. Although we may have grown apart as the years passed, I hold fond memories of seeing you all, every day at the office. Thank you for giving me something to look forward to on a daily basis. Frank Bastone, thank you for taking a chance on me—you've changed the trajectory of my life.

Martin Leatherman, thanks for always dreaming big with me and not conforming to society. Tom Brady (the teacher), Victor Bishop, and Sister Collette, it would have been easier for all of you not to take the time out of your day to talk some sense into me. It may not have seemed like it at the time, but I heard every word you said and I listened. Brett Blomme, Chris Dolen, and Maury Koffman—thank you for your friendship, guidance, and teaching me how to be successful in school.

Katie Spotz, I'm so lucky to have you as a friend. You are everything a friend should be—smart, supportive, and able to give good advice. You've steered me right so many times when I was going in the wrong direction and have talked me off the proverbial cliff. Thank you for being you and my Mr. Rogers.

To Second Sole in Lakewood, Ohio. Thank you for being more than just a running store. Bill, Tim, and John—it's because of you I'm able to run all these crazy races. To all my running friends, especially, Eric Lammers, Raj Rangoon, Paul Moore, Fred Kim, Chris Moore, Eric "Baby" Mooney, and Steve Hubbard, I wouldn't want to share the trails and miles with anyone else. All the friends I made out west while I was on my adventure—thank you.

Ebezner Fishwick, Sheriff Bernard, Dr. Hogginsnorff, Laney Bishop, and Simon Snifflensnocks, thank you for your stories and imagination.

Finally, John Mustard and Booker Brooks—thank you for believing in me, always.

CPSIA information can be obtained
at www.ICGtesting.com
Printed in the USA
LVHW041918210523
747621LV00003B/414